COLLECTING
FANS

Collecting
Fans

SUSAN MAYOR

CHRISTIE'S INTERNATIONAL COLLECTORS SERIES
MAYFLOWER BOOKS · NEW YORK CITY

In the same series:

Microscopes (Gerard L'Estrange Turner)
Phonographs and Gramophones (Christopher Proudfoot)
Victorian Ceramic Tiles (Julian Barnard)

Acknowledgements

Collecting is an agreeable disease. This book is designed as an introduction for would-be collectors and incipient experts. It is not a documented study, and therefore the bibliography has been made as comprehensive as possible. So many people have helped me – either through discussing their collections or by bringing their fans to Christie's South Kensington – that it is impossible to thank them all. However, I must single out Madeleine Ginsburg of the Victoria and Albert Museum; Hélène Alexander of the Fan Circle and Dr Van Eeghen, formerly of the Dutch State Archives, who commented on the text; and Christopher Lennox-Boyd who, as always, has been a mine of recondite information.

Text copyright © 1980 by Susan Mayor
Photographs copyright © 1980 by Christie's
South Kensington
Design Joop de Nijs gvn

All rights reserved under International and Pan American Copyright Convention. Published in the United States by Mayflower Books, Inc., 575 Lexington Avenue, New York City 10022. Originally published in England by Studio Vista, a division of Cassell Ltd., 35 Red Lion Square, London WC1R 4SG

Library of Congress Cataloging in Publication Data
Mayor, Susan.
    Fans.
    (Christie's international collectors series)
    Bibliography: pp. 115–118
    1. Fans – Collectors and collecting. I. Title.
II. Series.
NK4870.M3   736'.7'075   79-27103

ISBN: 0 8317 3199 0

First American edition 1980

Manufactured in Italy by
ⓐ AMILCARE PIZZI ARTI GRAFICHE S.p.A.
ⓑ CINISELLO B. (MILANO - ITALIA) - 1980

Abbreviations

CSK	Christie's South Kensington
S.E. and	(English)
S.F.	(foreign) indicate Lady Charlotte Schreiber's own catalogue numbers
S.M. and	(mounted)
S.U.	(unmounted) refer to numbers in Lionel Cust's catalogue of the Schreiber Collection

Contents

1   The Origins of the Fan

Fans are as old as hot weather. It is impossible to pinpoint where and when the fan originated. In hot climates it must always have been invaluable – in creating a breeze and keeping flies away – after all, the earliest known man comes from near the Equator. Later it became a work of art and was used in religious and royal ceremonies. Later still, it became the decorative accessory that we know today.

In its earliest form the fan was probably a small hand-sized screen – better and more effective than just fanning oneself with one's hands or a leaf. Handles were then added and these screens were adapted and decorated in numerous ways, using local materials and meeting demands and fashions as they arose.

The earliest fans are depicted in contemporary bas-reliefs, sculpture and painting. In Egypt fan-bearing courtiers carried semicircular feather fans on long poles. Some surviving examples have been found in tombs. That of Tutankhamen (1350 BC) contained one chased in gold with scenes of the young king hunting ostriches: their feathers would be used to decorate fans.

Early fans were also used for winnowing (separating the chaff from the grain), fly-swatting and starting fires.

Probably the earliest Chinese specimens of fans are two woven bamboo side-mounted fans (2nd century BC), excavated from the Mawangdui tomb near Changsha in Hunan province, but fans certainly existed in China long before that date.

Surviving examples of early fans are, of course, extremely rare and their history will have to be filled in gradually from contemporary painting, sculpture and literature.

In China, the first fans – handscreens – were probably of feathers, which would not have survived. At one stage peacock feathers were employed, then, to economize, silk was used and sometimes silk tapestry (*kesi*). They were sometimes curved at the tip to create a better breeze. Both sexes carried fans in China and detailed regulations accorded different types of fan to each rank of person. Gradually, more and more is being discovered about the origin of the folding fan. It is now thought that the brisé fan originated in Japan and was taken to China by a missionary (or traveller) in the 9th century. The folding fan was then adopted with alacrity, as it was obviously more convenient. When not in use it could be folded away in an embroidered silk fan case which, in turn, could be stored in the cuff, near the neck or in the boot, until next required.

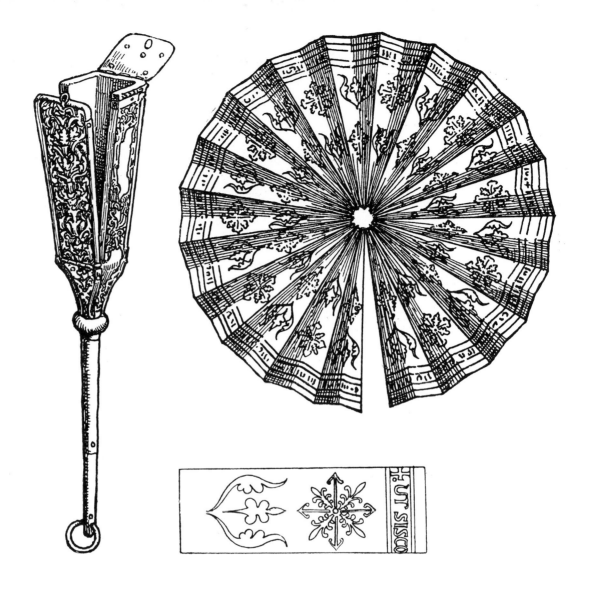

In China the fan was used in ceremonies and could also be used to shield one's face when passing dignitaries of equal rank – thus averting the necessity of endless greeting rituals.

The Western world's earliest surviving fan is preserved in the basilica of St. John the Baptist at Monza, 12 miles from Milan. There, in a domed octagonal treasury, can be seen the *flabellum* – or ceremonial fan – presented to the basilica by Theodolinda, the 6th-century Queen of the Lombards. This unique survival is made of purple vellum, decorated with gold and silver ornaments, like a similar later fan at Florence, known as the Tournus Flabellum, Queen Theodolinda's fan still retains its wooden box and silver-mounted handle. Strangely, it was not widely known until 1857, when its existence was publicized by the Victorian architect William Burges.

Queen Theodolinda's fan from a drawing by William Burges.

chimneypiece by Hugues Lallemend in the Hôtel de Cluny), and with hearts pierced by an arrow and a flaming torch. Bapst suggests that this fan dated from about 1580. The second fan, a little later in date, from the Sauvagest Collection, was larger (32 cm) and composed of a double leaf of découpé vellum with mica and silk inserted between the leaves. At the time (1881), Bapst knew of other examples, including those in the collections of Mme Jubinal and M. Dupont Auberville. Woolliscroft Rhead, however, suggests that the Jubinal fan was 17th-century.

A very similar fan from the collection of Miss Esther Oldham is illustrated in Nancy Armstrong's *Collector's History of Fans*. It is probably the one Miss Oldham has since given to the Boston Museum.

From Pierre de l'Estoile's *l'Isle des Hermaphrodites* (1588), Bapst quotes a passage describing Henri III using a similar fan: On lui mettoit à la main droite (à Henri III) un instrument qui s'estendait et se reploit en y donnant seulement un coup de doigt que nous appelons ici un esvantail: il estoit d'un velin aussi delicatement découpé qu'il estoit possible, avec de la dentelle à l'entour de pareille étoffe. Il estoit grand, car cela devoit servir comme d'un parasol pour se conserver une hâsle, et pour donner quelque refraichissement, à ce teint délicat... Tous ceux que je pus voir aux autres chambres en avaient un aussi de mesme étoffe, ou de taffetas avec de la dentelle d'or et d'argent à l'entour.

A taffeta fan of the period, believed to have belonged to Mary, Queen of Scots, survives in the National Museum of Antiquities for Scotland, but it is a cockade fan with sliding tortoiseshell sticks, the leaf of bands of green, yellow and brown silk and silver lace. There is a rectangular handscreen mount of pierced parchment (Italian, c. 1570–80) illustrated in Seligman and Hughes, *Domestic Needlework* (plate 48) from the collection of Albert Figdor.

By the second half of the 17th century most fans were about 12 in. long, with a wide span of almost 180°, painted kid leaves and either ivory or tortoiseshell sticks, more or less touching, simply carved and pierced, and just tapering gently from the tip to the pivot. However, two fine examples of mica fans of this period are known; these have a slightly smaller span. One was sold at Christie's 1969 (see illustration p. 8) and a similar one is in the Messel Collection. It is amazing that an object composed of so many small segments should have survived so long. They were made from many painted panes of mica joined by painted strips of paper to the sticks. This all shows how carefully designed a fan has to be. Not only does it have to look decorative, it has to be practical to use, to be perfectly balanced so that it is comfortable to hold, and to open and close. It is, of course, the pleated paper fan that is the most conventional.

In 1765, Diderot published *Recueil de Planches sur les Sciences, les Arts Libéraux et les Arts Méchaniques* to illustrate his encyclopaedia. The four plates on fanmaking illustrate clearly the routine in a fan workshop. It is interesting to note that all the workers illustrated are women. A very large proportion of women were employed in the fan trade in the 18th century.

The first plate shows a large well-lit workroom with five women preparing the paper for the leaves. The first girl stands at a large L-shaped table with a pile of sheets of paper, still rectangular, a bowl of glue and an sponge. She glues two sheets together which the second girl then stretches on a fanshaped frame. The third then hangs the frame from the rafters. The fourth takes the frames down when dry and removes the papers from the frame, piles the frames up and hands the paper to a fifth girl who trims them to a fan shape. The stages are all numbered and explained in a key and below them are scale drawings of the equipment: the

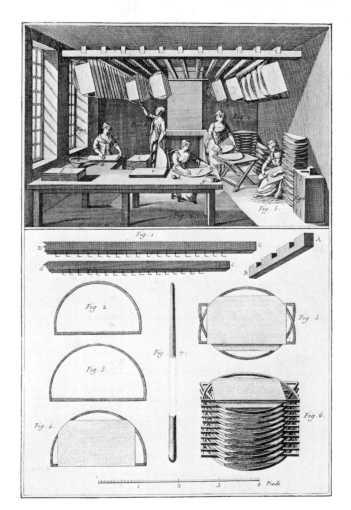
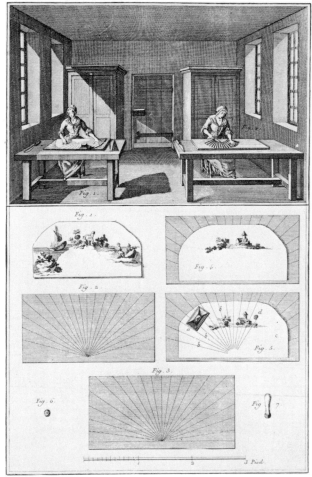

Le Travail de l'Eventailliste from
Diderot's Encyclopédie 1765.

11

Fan, the leaf painted with drunken Bacchus, the reverse with a classical ruin; the blonde tortoiseshell sticks piqué in gold with Diana and cupids. Italian, second quarter of 18th century. 11 in. (Photograph by courtesy of Christie's South Kensington.)

Fan, the chickenskin leaf painted with the Bay of Naples by Francesco Petilli, inscribed Veduta di Napoli col ritorno della squadra da Livorno; the reverse (illustrated) with figures from an Etruscan vase; the tortoiseshell sticks posé with red gold. Neapolitan, late 18th century. 11 in. Now in the Glasgow Museum. (Photograph by courtesy of Christie's South Kensington.)

frames or *rondes,* and the *sonde* or probe which will be used later, and which resembles a small billiard cue about 14 in. long. There is also a 'stone' and mallet used for gilding fan leaves. Mrs Alexander, President of the Fan Circle, points out that the stone is probably an agate, which is used by gilders to smoothe and brighten gold leaf. The second plate illustrates the fan painter, also female. She sits alone in a grander room at a large bureau with the fan leaf flat in front of her. On an easel in front stands the picture she is copying.

Plates 3 and 4 show the next stage, the mounting of the fans – a very exacting task. Two women sit at large tables with large cupboards to store the finished fans in behind them. The first woman works out where the creases are to go. To do so, she lays the leaf on a large walnut board, etched with radiating grooves. She has more than one of these boards and selects the most suitable for the eventual span of the fan, arranging it carefully so that creases do not cut across the design at the wrong or ugly places. Then with a tool called a *jeton* – about an inch in diameter, with or without a handle and made of silver or copper – she creases the fan by running the *jeton* along the paper above the grooves. Next the centre semi-circle of the leaf is cut out and the leaf is pleated like a concertina along the lines already marked. Then the second girl with the probe or *sonde* eases apart the two layers of paper between the folds at the bottom edge of the fan to insert the sticks, or rather the plain extensions to the sticks that one never sees on a finished fan. Although it is possible the sticks were made in another part of the same workshop, it is equally possible that they were imported from as far away as China. Before mounting the leaf on the sticks, the leaf is folded up tightly and trimmed at either end. The sticks are then slid into place and a band of paper is bound round the outer edge of the leaf.

Another good illustration of the tools used by the fanmaker is the trade card of the Dutch fanmaker Frans Beenevelt de Jonge. These, therefore, are all the manoeuvres which have to be performed in preparing a folding fan. Not all fans had double leaves: late 17th- and early 18th-century Italian and Flemish fans seldom do. Fans with single leaves are often said to be 'monté à l'anglais', probably because, as paper taxes were high, the English had to be even more economical than elsewhere.

The fan illustrated by Diderot was just a straightforward simple fan. As we shall see now, they were not always so, and often countless other details had to be added.

By the beginning of the 18th century the sticks had begun to be decorated. Both ivory and tortoiseshell sticks were often *piqué* with small studs or strips of silver or gold (CSK, Baldwin Coll., 4 May 1978, lot 27, £320: see opposite plate). The finest *piqué* is said to have been done in Paris and Naples, but it was also practised in England and Holland. Late in the 18th century *posé d'or* was occasionally used, that is, tortoiseshell inlaid with chased gold designs (CSK, 31 October 1978, lot 13, £340: see illustration opposite). At this point some sticks begin to be *clouté* with mother-of-pearl (CSK, Baldwin Coll., 4 May 1978, lot 100, £2,600; also lot 45 in the same sale, £410), often in the form of Harlequin or other figures from the Commedia dell'Arte (CSK, Baldwin Coll., 4 May 1978, lot 34, £170, c. 1710: see illustration) or, as in the sale of 17 May 1979 (lot 5), birds. Another combination is found on an Italian mid-18th-century fan (Baldwin Coll., lot 3, £100); the ivory sticks have mother-of-pearl guards *clouté* with tortoiseshell. Another type of stick to be found in the first half of the 18th century is of stained ivory; sometimes only the guardsticks are stained. One Italian fan sold at Christie's had its ivory guardsticks stained red with veins in a jigsaw-seaweed motif to resemble marble.

Fan, the leaf painted with an allegory of the permanence of marriage, with gods and putti; the ivory sticks carved, clouté with mother-of-pearl and piqué with silver, the guardsticks with applied mother-of-pearl Harlequins and dolphins c. 1710. 11 in. (Photograph by courtesy of Christie's South Kensington.)

Most of these sticks from the first half of the 18th century are narrower and trimmer than those of the previous century. They now tend to have a slight neck and *gorge* – that is, the guardsticks taper gently from the tip to where the mount ends and then bulge slightly to form curved shoulders and taper again to the pivot. It is normal for the sticks to spread out again at the pivot to form a handle. By about 1740 the handle is sometimes carved to form a shell or a sheaf of corn or some other decorative object. A Dutch fan in the CSK sale of 17 May 1979 (lot 19) formed a bird's head. Then and also later in the century it is quite normal for the guardsticks to be spliced with another material at the handle, such as ivory with tortoiseshell or mother-of-pearl, wood with bone. This is both strengthening and decorative. Occasionally the guardsticks are made of a different material from the other sticks; for example, tortoiseshell guardsticks and ivory sticks. The normal span of a fan of this period is about 120°, whereas late 17th-century fans were almost 180°. Again, the sticks still touch when fully open to form a continuous surface.

Where were all these sticks made? It is still not fully known. Most ivory is thought to have been worked in Paris, then towards the end of the 18th century in Dieppe, but since many of the craftsmen were Protestants some must have fled to London and Holland after the revocation of the Edict of Nantes (see Chapter 3). Certainly many of the members of the Fanmakers Company describe themselves as stickmakers.

Throughout the century many sticks were imported from China. Most of the trade with China was by way of France and England. Holland is not thought to have imported many fans from China – individual sailors may have brought them back, and in 1760 the Dutch East India Company is known to have sent a sample or samples to Canton for copying; this was a commercial failure, but Dr van Eeghen has suggested that the subject of one sample was Perseus and Andromeda, as a number of Chinese versions of a form of this subject have turned up in Holland. At this stage it is still too early to know, but probably most European sticks were made in France, England and the simpler sticks in Holland, and possibly some of the *piqué* sticks in Italy.

By mid-century the guardsticks are more decorated – a superb damaged fan (CSK, 23 October 1979) had sticks decorated with mica, hardstones and chased silver – others are composed of ivory, or ivory and mother-

Fan, the leaf painted with a central vignette of Zeus and Danae, flanked by putti and expressive heads; the ivory sticks carved and pierced with urns of flowers, guitar shapes and putti. French, c. 1780. 9¾ in.; in glazed gilt fan case. (Photograph by courtesy of Christie's South Kensington.)

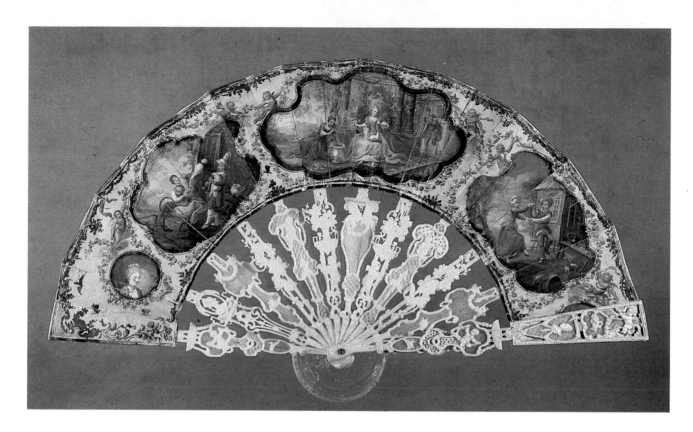

Wedding fan, the leaf painted with portrait miniatures of the bride and groom and three shaped vignettes of courtship, against a pink ground; the ivory battoire sticks carved and pierced. French, probably for the Spanish market, c. 1780. 10½ in. (Photograph by courtesy of Christie's South Kensington: 23 October 1979, lot 68, £ 320.)

of-pearl, carved and backed with coloured tinsels or decorated with straw-work.

In the middle of the century, the shoulders of the guardsticks are more often squared off, not rounded as before. However, they are now often arranged the opposite way, that is, the upper half of the guardstick is broader than the lower half but it is also squared off. The sticks are now often spaced out when open and most fans of this period (1750–80) have a wide span, almost 180° or even over 180° or *à grand vol*. During this rococo period sticks cease to be carved all alike and they are carved with great movement and gusto, with figures, flowers and rocaille, the pattern moving across several sticks.

From the end of this period date the *battoire* sticks. These are, again, ornamental sticks, spread out and with large decorative pierced medallions in the centre. The medallions are sometimes in the shape of tennis rackets, or of guitars (CSK, Baldwin Coll., 4 May 1978,

lot 116, £550: see illustration opposite). *Battoire* sticks are always thought to have been much favoured by the Spanish market; certainly there were a number of examples in the 1920 Madrid Exhibition.

Most sticks are either entirely of ivory or of mother-of-pearl. They are usually elaborately carved and pierced with figures and flowers. On the more important fans the carving normally echoes the theme of the leaf. For special commissions, both the sticks and the leaf would have been specially designed and ordered. This is a useful point, as a great number of fans have been remounted on later sticks, or vice versa, because

15

either the sticks or the mount have been damaged. Many sticks, both mother-of-pearl and ivory, are backed with a thin layer of mother-of-pearl. The guardsticks often have a thin layer sandwiched between their two outer layers; it glistens through the carved pierced sections of the top layer as it does when backing the sticks. Both the ivory and mother-of-pearl sticks are usually silvered and gilt and often painted as well. Sometimes they are even decorated with straw-work (Christie's, 23 February 1972, lot 171, 220 gns: see illustration; a very elaborate example). The straw-work is even stained various colours. The sticks are also

cloutè with mother-of-pearl. Silver and gold *piqué*-work no longer seems to occur at this period. At this period the sticks are also backed with coloured tinsels or coloured metallic paper, mainly strawberry pink, or occasionally with mica. Sticks of tortoiseshell and of horn also occur occasionally, as do stained wooden sticks, although they are more frequently seen in the last two decades of the century. At this time too, one sometimes finds sticks of alternating materials or contrasting colours – wood and ivory or stained and non-stained ivory. But this happened much more frequently on mid-19th-century Chinese export fans, where one might find three contrasting materials, for example, mother-of-pearl, ivory and cloisonné enamel or silver filigree. From about the 1760s date the sticks called 'Pagoda' by Woolliscroft Rhead. They are of pierced ivory carved to resemble bundles of rods. No. 119 in the 1920 Madrid Exhibition was a fine example; another example

Fine fan, the silk leaf painted with figures and flowers within formal arbours of straw-work, mother-of-pearl and sequins; the ivory sticks carved, pierced, silvered, gilt and clouté with mother-of-pearl and straw-work trophies. Probably German, c. 1770. 10½ in.; framed and glazed. (Photograph by courtesy of Christie's.)

Fan, the leaf painted with a country fair, the reverse with lovers in a landscape; the ivory sticks pierced and painted, closing to form bundles of rods held by retaining rings. French, c. 1760. 11½ in. (Photograph by courtesy of Christie's South Kensington.)

was CSK, Baldwin Coll., 4 May 1978, lot 91 (£360: see illustration). Each stick is divided in two lengthwise, joined only at intervals, and so the closed fan does resemble a bundle of rods, not really very Chinese in style, but more like some chairs of the period with legs called Pagoda legs; the chapter on chinoiserie in *Fans from the East* mentioned similar designs in Charles Manwaring's *Designs for Furniture* (1760). A set of these chairs was sold at Christie's recently.

By about 1780, sticks became simpler again. Most fans span about 120°. Certainly many of the printed fans have straight narrow plain wooden sticks with a rectangular projection at the tip when they join the mount; they are normally about 11 in. long. A number of European fans are mounted on Chinese sticks, sometimes ivory, sometimes wood, and decorated with fretwork. Indeed, the main decoration on late 18th-century sticks is this pierced work, executed both in Dieppe and in China, and perhaps in Eng-

land too. Some of the fans have plain sticks with just pierced work on the upper, broader part of the guardsticks. On some fans the sticks are now touching again to form a solid surface, possibly because it was at this stage that brisé fans returned to fashion (brisé fans being those with no separate leaf – the sticks are extended to form the leaf). Some guardsticks were decorated with cut-steel beads. A superb fan illustrated in *Fans from the East* (plate 16) has guards set with Jasperware plaques. The brisé fan painted with vignettes, possibly by Angelica Kauffmann, had guardsticks set with enamelled portrait miniatures (Christie's, 28 July 1971, lot 55,

420 gns: see illustration). The sticks, as in some of the more important fans, are not straight but slightly tapered and slightly shaped. These elaborately decorated guard-sticks are an advance guard of some of the very elaborate trimmings to be found on early 19th-century French printed fans.

These early 19th-century French printed fans (c. 1815–25) are normally about 8½ in. long with a span of about 120°. Their sticks are touching, normally of ivory or bone, shaped in a rather angular way, pierced and *clouté* with steel, sequins or mother-of-pearl. The guardsticks are often very elaborate, and can be set with mother-of-pearl plaques, coral, opals and gilt metal plaques. An example sold at CSK (17 May 1979, lot 87, £135) was set with enamelled clockfaces.

Fans remain small whilst dresses remain thin and hoopless, getting bigger in the 1830s and 1850s when skirts grow wider and pockets are again larger.

By the mid-19th century the finest fans usually have mother-of-pearl sticks. Again, they are touching but the fans tend to measure about 10 in. and have a span of nearly 180°. The sticks are often very wide, with rounded shoulders tapering to the pivot. The tip of the guardsticks is normally fairly straight and the same length as the mount, which is often quite short, some-times only about a third of the total length of the fan. They are elaborately carved, pierced, gilt and backed with mother-of-pearl as in the 18th century.

The less expensive sticks are of ivory, bone or lacquered wood. Some sticks are even decorated with lithographic scenes. At this

Fine ivory brisé fan, painted with two oval vignettes of the Shepherdess of the Alps, and Gualtherius and Griselda, possibly by Angelica Kauffmann, R.A., on either side of a rectangular carved and pierced plaque of Venus in a lion-drawn chariot with putti; the reserves delicately carved, pierced and gilt with flowers, hearts and other amatory devices; the guardsticks with two enamel miniatures in gold frames. c. 1780. 10 in. (one guardstick repaired). (Photograph by courtesy of Christie's.)

period one begins to find gilt metal handles attached to the pivot, often with elaborate silk tassels suspended from them (CSK, 17 July 1979, lot 149: see colour plate – a very fine example). One does come across 18th-century fans with handles, but so far the ones I have seen have always been added in the 19th century by M. Duvelleroy or some other *éventailliste*. Dr van Eeghen tells me that her father owned a design for an 18th-century fan handle but she, too, has never come across an example. (Since writing this passage, an 18th-century fan with contemporary handle has arrived at CSK for sale on 31 January 1980.)

Fan, the narrow leaf a hand-coloured lithograph of a court scene in 17th-century style, the reverse with the gods on Olympus; the mother-of-pearl sticks carved, pierced and set with a central vignette of a hand-coloured lithograph of figures in 18th-century dress in a park and two smaller vignettes painted with bunches of flowers, the guardsticks set with porcelain plaques painted with putti within elaborate enamelled gilt metal mounts also set with two mirrors; with an elaborate handle. c. 1860. (Photograph by courtesy of Christie's South Kensington.)

Fan, the gauze leaf painted with blue and white daisies, trimmed with ribbons loosely tacked to form rosettes when the fan is closed; with carved and painted wooden sticks. c. 1890. 14 in. (Photograph by courtesy of Christie's South Kensington.)

Between 1860 and 1870 sticks grow a little longer, a little narrower and with slightly more angular shoulders. They are also plainer, normally bone with a slight pierced pattern. The expensive lace fans tend to have mother-of-pearl or tortoiseshell sticks. By the 1880s and 1890s sticks are often very long, about 12 in. They tend to be narrower, spaced out and tapering from the tips to the pivot. The ends of the guards often have a little carved floral decoration echoed round the tips of the sticks. They no longer have shoulders. Many are of wood, lacquered white, grey or black.

There are a number of fans of that period which have rather light shaped and curved sticks, such as CSK, 17 May 1979, lot 147 (£40; see colour plate).

In the 20th century, the printed fans normally have plain wooden sticks. The feather fans normally have mother-of-pearl sticks if white or coloured, and tortoiseshell if black. The handles of the ostrich plumes popular in the 1920s were normally of stained ivory.

In September 1922 the magazine *Art, Goût, Beauté* mentions long heavy tortoiseshell brisé fans with wide sticks as being fashionable.

Now to revert to the mounts. As will be seen in Chapter 3, until about 1780 they were normally of vellum or paper. The more valuable were sometimes embellished with many of the same materials as the sticks, namely mica in the late 17th century and the mid-18th century, and straw-work and mother-of-pearl in the mid-18th century. To this one can add spangles in the early 18th century (CSK, 17 May 1979, lot 13, £60: see colour plate), feathers, occasionally butterfly wings, and applied silks in the mid-18th century. A little later, when many of the leaves were of silk, they were trimmed with gold braid, sequins, spangles again, and even occasionally had painted ivory faces, as will be seen in the Canton fans of the 19th century described in Chapter 6.

Some fans were of silvered paper, particularly from about the mid-18th century to the 1780s. This was often decorated with cut-paper or *découpé* work. Others were decorated with bands of pressed silver paper.
The fans with spy holes had insertions of gut.
Occasionally one finds 18th-century lace fans. There is a fine example at Waddesdon; another was sold at CSK 29 July 1976 (lot 34, £140), but the lace was re-grounded. Lot 8 (c. 1780) in the same sale, which realized

Fan, the gauze leaf decorated overall with mica painted with vignettes of La Vie Rustique; the ivory sticks gilt, the guardsticks of tortoiseshell clouté with mother-of-pearl and coloured marbles. French, c. 1700. 11½ in. (Photograph by courtesy of Christie's South Kensington.)

Fan, the leaf painted with a shepherd and shepherdess and decorated with spangles of eagles, flowers and putti; with ivory sticks and tortoiseshell guardsticks. English, c. 1720. 10 in. (Photograph by courtesy of Christie's South Kensington.)

Black lace fan; the tortoiseshell sticks carved with the monogram UB with a coronet above. c. 1880. 13 in. (Photograph by courtesy of Christie's South Kensington.)

£135, also had a lace mount set with painted vignettes. In the same sale there were two French fans of darned muslin, c. 1760 (lots 43 and 44), which realized £170 and £150 respectively.

It was not until the 1860s that lace was used in quantity on fans, and some very fine examples survive. White lace was mounted on mother-of-pearl sticks, black lace on tortoiseshell sticks (CSK, 17 May 1979, lot 27, £20: see colour plate).

The mounts were made 'à disposition', to the correct shape for the fan. Obviously examples of varying quality survive. The lace used is mainly Brussels, Honiton and Chantilly. Some of the finest examples are worked with scenes. A fine fan sold at Sotheby's Belgravia in May 1979 was worked with scenes from *Don Quixote*.

There are also some rare examples of 17th- and 18th-century embroidered fans, and there is a mid-18th-century Dresden-work fan leaf in the Cooper-Hewitt Museum, New York.

In G.S.Seligman and T.Hughes, *Domestic Needlework*, several examples of embroidered fans are illustrated: Colour Plate XVIIB: a fan screen embroidered with a vignette of a pelican in its piety with a silver border, French, late 17th-century. Plate 47A, B and C: a pair of needlework handscreens of upturned pear-shape worked in coloured wools with chinoiserie figures like chair covers of the period, English, c. 1720, from

22

the Percival Griffiths Collection; and a single handscreen, similar. Plate 48C: another handscreen also worked in petit-point, with a shepherdess, English, c. 1740. There are also two interesting examples from later in the century. Colour Plate XVIIA: an unmounted fan leaf of gauze embroidered with David and the head of Goliath and vignettes of fountains, against an unworked·ground, probably Italian, c. 1775–1800. Plate 46A: a linen leaf embroidered in silver and coloured silks with three oval landscapes and delicate floral reserves, Italian, c. 1780–1800.

In the 1760s sequins and braid were often embroidered round painted vignettes on silk fan leaves. Early in the 19th century gold, lace and sequins became more and more prominent on French fans, including those for the Spanish market. These fans, profusely embroidered with sequins, were revived in a similar style in the early 20th century. This time, however, the ground was usually completely covered with sequins, no longer normally gold but of various bright colours, sometimes with mother-of-pearl sticks stained to match the sequins.

From the 1840s one finds pairs of handscreens embroidered in beadwork like the footstools of the period. They are often circular, trimmed with fringes and with turned wooden handles.

Fan Boxes

One of the reasons many fans have survived in such fine condition is that they have sometimes been stored in boxes, occasionally their original boxes. Many of the English 18th-century fan boxes retain the fanmaker's label. It is, therefore, beginning to be possible to recognize some fanmakers' boxes. Clarke favoured boxes of hexagonal section covered in green paper and overpainted. Most 18th-century boxes to survive are of papier mâché lined with old

newspapers. The English boxes are all long canisters with a removable cap either hexagonal or elliptical. They are covered in pink, white, blue, red and orange figured paper; some English boxes are also covered in French paper. Dutch boxes are long narrow rectangular boxes with lids covered in paper of various colours figured with stencilled motifs, often in a simple cross pattern.

Tapering rectangular boxes with hooks and hinges covered in shagreen have also survived, and occasionally French or English late 18th-century oval tubular boxes of red morocco. The collector must beware of oval paper tubular boxes covered with imitation scarlet leather; these date from the 1840s, as can be seen from the typography of the paper used in the papier mâché. A box, formerly in the collection of Lady Charlotte Schreiber, sold at Sotheby's Belgravia in May 1979 contained an act of Parliament of 8 Victoria (i.e. 1845).

In the 19th century most of the boxes that survive are of the same type as Dutch 18th-century ones, but they are often hinged. Regency boxes, however, are often rectangular versions of English 18th-century boxes. There are also some fine morocco coffin-shaped French fan boxes of this type from about 1810. From the 1840s boxes are mainly covered in printed paper, but sometimes wooden and lined with quilted satin. By the 1880s most of the boxes are now domed and are covered in white, black or pink satin, lined with matching paper, with the fanmaker's label stamped in gold inside the lid. Canton fans have the grander and lacquered boxes, but many of the finest ostrich feather fans by Duvelleroy come in enormous rectangular white satin or white paper fitted boxes.

A number of late 19th-century tooled leather boxes also survive. There are also a number of boxes, probably early 20th century, covered in 18th-century and later silks; they often bear Spanish labels.

*Fan, the black leaf painted with putti attending to
the toilet of a prince, the reverse with bunches of
flowers; the tortoiseshell sticks carved and pierced.
North European, late 17th century. (Photograph by
courtesy of Christie's South Kensington.)*

3

Seventeenth- and eighteenth-century Painted Fans

Baroque

It is unlikely that the collector today will come across fans earlier than the second half of the 17th century. However, in the thirteen years of specialized fan sales at Christie's, about two dozen fans dating from the last few decades of the 17th century have come on the market and so it should be possible for the serious collector to be able to include at least one in a collection.

So far three types have emerged. The first is a very long fan (12 in.) painted on a thick, coarse kid leaf with a wide span of nearly 180°, painted all over with a rather loose but well-balanced composition normally incorporating fat putti, in bright colours often enhanced with gold, such as 'The Toilette of a Prince' (CSK, Baldwin Coll., 4 May 1978, lot 80, £800: see illustration). These fans have rather heavy tortoiseshell sticks with sparse decoration. In fact, the sticks are almost always identical in shape although sometimes of ivory rather than tortoiseshell. They probably come from the same source. There are fan leaves of this type in the Schreiber Collection (in fact, they hover between this and the next type in style: the subjects are similar to the first but they are less elaborate than the second), such as (S.M. 359 and S.F. 2): a French fan leaf painted with an allegory of the marriage of Louis XIV. The scene is painted as if planned as a rectangle and cut down to a fan shape, sometimes cutting across arches, which

gives the fan a very theatrical air. The ladies-in-waiting are holding fans and cupids are making the bed.

(S.U. 360): 'The Lovers' Agency' – in a classical building on an island lovers approach tables covered in green cloth and are presented with cards inscribed 'Congé pour un Amant Constant, etc.'

(S.U. 361 and S.F. 3): 'The Toilet', painted with a lady at her toilet in a room steeped and scattered with flowers as her lover enters. (S.U. 362): 'The Bride' – again, a very open stage-set-like arrangement containing a large four-poster bed. The young bride is embraced by the groom as attendants undress her. By the door friends receive the priest.

In the Walker Collection there were two further fans of this type but with classical scenes of Diana and Endymion and the chariot of Phoebus. Here the bottom edge is painted with flowers.

In this group of fans there are a number which are much simpler, depicting perhaps just pots of orange trees surmounted by putti and drapes. Some of these have been catalogued simply as North European, others, the more elaborate ones, as French. The second type is far superior in quality. It is almost certainly French and depicts very elaborate scenes filled with figures – all well painted. Their costumes in particular are superbly handled. As the previous type, they are painted in bodycolour, usually on a dark ground, but on a thinner kid leaf of the type called chickenskin. A fan leaf of this type was sold at Christie's (3 May 1972, 230 gns: see illustration) and is now in the Victoria and Albert Museum; and there is an enchanting series in the Musée des Arts Décoratifs and the Musée Carnavalet of market and other everyday Paris views. These all tend to be longer than the fans of the next few decades.

The third type is of mica and much smaller in size than the two previous categories. Several examples of this type are known. One (Christie's, Bompas Coll., 14 July 1969, lot 98, 260 gns: see illustration p. 8) is painted with peacocks, busts and flowers, and has tortoiseshell sticks. Another is in the Messel Collection. The fans echo the construction of the late 16th-century fan described by Bapst. The painted panes of mica are held in place by paper frames. Each slice of mica is painted with a brightly coloured jewel-like miniature, a figure, a bust with elaborate hairstyle, an animal or flowers. Those, too, were probably French.

Since figures in contemporary dress appear in most of the scenes, as usual the best way of dating them is by the fashion of the costumes or hairstyles.

Many more fans survive from the early years of the 18th century, and hence there are more to compare and assess. It is possible to sort them into groups but it is still not always, or even often, possible to be certain of their country of origin. The chief way of dating and attributing all painted fans of the 17th, 18th and 19th centuries is by the style of painting, that is, by trying to compare it with watercolours, portrait miniatures and oil paintings that have already been ascribed a country of origin and a date. There are many things that make this a difficult task. The manufacture of fans was fairly widespread and the trade ever more so. There was much importing and exporting of both whole fans and fan parts. Also, many fans were not well painted, but executed by journeymen and hack-painters, and

very little about them has been discovered, although gradually gleanings from contemporary local newspapers, registrations at town halls, insurance policies and wills are beginning to unravel a pattern. We have seen that sticks were often made elsewhere from the mount. But there is another equally confusing point. As in oil painting, a fan leaf was not necessarily painted by one person alone. There are several examples where the borders appear to be Chinese and the central design European. But even more like portrait paintings, where some artists are known to have been specialists and to have painted only the heads whilst one assistant painted the hands and another the drapes or background (for example, Sir Godfrey Kneller always called himself 'face-painter' and for most of his practice employed Capt. Byng to provide compositions and stances, Alexander van Haecken to paint the drapes, and sundry dog and cat painters to paint other relevant parts), this certainly happened with fans. Dr van Eeghen has found instances where Dutch fan workshops employed artists who specialized in flowers and in faces and were employed just to finish off these parts of fans. The reverse of the fan is almost always painted in a weaker style by a lesser artist.

By the third quarter of the 17th century Paris and Versailles were becoming the centre for fashionable and luxury taste, a position Paris has held on and off ever since. In 1673 an Association des Eventaillistes was formed with the King as patron. To qualify as a member the fanmaker was required to serve four years' apprenticeship, and some to produce a *chef d'œuvre*. The entrance fee was 400 livres. Widows could inherit their husband's membership if they did not remarry. There were 60 founder members. When the Edict of Nantes was revoked in 1685, the Protestant members fled to London and Holland, but by 1753 the Association des Eventaillistes had increased again to 150 members.

Fan leaf, painted with people of fashion embarking upon a ferry boat, the reverse with bunches of flowers. c. 1680. 20 in. Now in the Victoria & Albert Museum, London. (Photograph by courtesy of Christie's.)

Dismounted fan leaf, painted with the Triumph of Venus. c. 1720; in English decorated frame with framer's label, c. 1740. In the collection of the Hon. C. A. Lennox-Boyd. (Photograph by courtesy of Christie's South Kensington.)

In England, too, the trade became organized when in 1709 the Worshipful Company of Fanmakers was granted its Charter by Queen Anne, the last purely trade City company to be formed. There were apparently 200 to 500 people sufficiently involved in the business living in London or Westminster or within a 20-mile radius at that time; probably some were French refugees. Sadly, the minutes only survive from 1747 with the enrolment of the 39th member. On 1 July 1751, Thomas Coe, stickmaker, Bethnal Green, was admitted as a member. No. 882, Francis Chassereau, Jr., was admitted as fanmaker 3 November 1755; No. 883,

Robert Clarke, 12 September 1755, at Mr Clarke's in Bell Sauvage Yard, Ludgate Hill; No. 936, Sarah Ashton, 1 February 1770. The Company's motto is 'Arts and Trade Unite'. They still flourish today, although they are obviously more concerned with engineering on an industrial scale.

So we have on one side the French protecting their trade with the Association des Eventaillistes and, on the other side of the Channel, the Company of Fanmakers. Whilst England and France were exporting many fans, they were also importing a large number, particularly from the East at the turn of the 17th and 18th centuries. The Chinese taste was the vogue. European fans from the beginning of the 18th century often show influences of the Chinese taste, particularly on brisé fans, which make their appearance in Europe at this time. In Savary de Brulou's *Dictionnaire Universelle de Commerce* (1723) under 'Eventail': Les Eventails de la Chine et ceux de l'Angleterre qui les imitent si parfaitement, sont les plus en vogue; Et il faut avouer que les uns ont un si beau lacque, et que les autres cédent aux beaux Eventails de France, ils leur sont au moins préférables par ces deux qualités. Unfortunately, we do not know to which type of English fan he refers, as very few fans surviving from the early 18th century have been identified as English. This may, of course, apply to Chinese fan leaves mounted in England, as he admits he cannot tell the difference between Chinese and English fans, or rather that English fans imitate Chinese fans so well.

Now to return to the types that have an identified country of origin. France continues to produce superbly painted fans, on paper leaves and on chickenskin, until about 1735 still very much High Baroque in style, on dark grounds with mythological or theatrical subjects and pretty flowers on the reverse. The sticks became neater and were often *clouté* with mother-of-pearl plaques. The fans have become a little shorter than in the last century.

In Italy, the main subjects were classical (CSK, Baldwin Coll., 4 May 1978, lot 27, £ 320: see colour plate p. 12). They were also often taken from famous Roman paintings such as Guido Reni's *Aurora*. Thus they were very suitable gifts to bring back from a Grand Tour. Early in the century they were also Biblical (Christie's, 11 July 1967, lot 173, 25 gns, painted with a Nativity, c. 1720). They are often on very fine chickenskin. A number of Italian fans have been signed and inscribed, which is a great help in identifying them but would be of even more use had these painters been recorded elsewhere. These fans were not only sold retail to tourists and to the rich Italian nobility, but also exported in quantity, particularly to England. For instance, Christie's, 3 May 1972 (lot 86, 30 gns): Diana and attendants resting, by Leonardo Germo of Rome, $10\frac{3}{4}$ in. long. Another fan by the same artist of the 'Triumph of Mordecai' was exhibited in the 1870 South Kensington Museum Exhibition and is now in the Victoria and Albert Museum. An interesting group of three fan leaves was sold at Christie's (21 October 1970, lots 298: see illustra-

An interesting documented fan design: pen and ink drawing of Venus and Adonis in a panoramic landscape with villas and castles, signed Dominico Spinetti, Napolitano, Roma F. c. 1720. $10\frac{1}{4}$ in.; in contemporary wood box inscribed A. Sigri Baracchi and Mucotti, Livorno. Now in the Victoria & Albert Museum, London. (Photograph by courtesy of Christie's.)

tion on previous page; 299 and 300) in their original fanshaped box for export via Leghorn, and two are now in the Victoria and Albert Museum, Department of Prints and Drawings. One is a drawing in black ink; other examples exist in red ink. It is possible that many of these fan leaves were mounted in England on arrival.

Another type that survives occasionally is the early 18th-century *découpé* fan of vellum. There is a fine example in the Messel Collection (see Peter Thornton in *Antiques International,* ill. 7). This has a central painted classical cartouche and several small vignettes; the remaining ground is of kid *découpé* to resemble lace. The sticks are more elaborate than those on their French counterparts at that time; they are pierced and carved and are no longer more or less straight, but have a bulbous shape at their necks.

Also at the turn of the 17th and 18th cen-

turies the brisé fan appears in Europe. As far as has been established, they appear to have have been produced only in France and in Holland, the French versions being the type that collectors of fans describe as Vernis Martin – a term which owes its name to the shiny lacquer-like varnish applied to the painting. They vary in quality but are often superb. They are smaller than other fans of the period and are painted with both classical and theatrical scenes, using the sticks as if there were a separate mount. At the *gorge* sometimes is a narrow border, usually painted with small chinoiserie scenes. The other type, probably Dutch, is more lightly painted on a central medallion and the reserves are pierced to produce Baroque scrollwork. The first type, in particular, was very popular in the second half of the 19th century and the collector may be confused by reproductions or heavy restoration, especially as a small handful of undecorated fans still survive.

Rococo

By 1735, there is a preference for lighter, more rococo styles, and painted and printed leaves are prefered to the brisé. In France subjects are now often pastoral and romantic. The leaves now span out to almost a semicircle, having been about 120° at the beginning of the century. They are now always painted on light grounds and the sticks have become a much more important entity. These are predominately of ivory or mother-of-pearl and elaborately carved. Although designs on leaves cover the whole mount, it is at this stage that the designs begin to be broken up into vignettes (CSK, Baldwin Coll., 4 May 1978, lot 90, £470: see colour plate). There is a series of fans, probably Flemish, where the leaf is divided asymmetrically, often by a border of rocaille decorated with glitter, into two compartments differing greatly in size (CSK, 31 October 1978, lot 3, £150: see illustration).

Fan, the leaf painted with scenes at harvest time and decorated with glitter; the ivory sticks painted and clouté with mother-of-pearl. Flemish, c. 1750. 10¼ in. (Photograph by courtesy of Christie's South Kensington.)
Below: Fan, the leaf painted with L'Enseigne de Gersaint, after Watteau, the reverse with lovers in a landscape; the ivory sticks carved, pierced, painted, gilt and backed with tinsel. French, c. 1730. 11½ in. The right side of the composition is in reverse. M. Gersaint's shop sign is now in the Schloss Charlottenburg, Berlin. (Photograph by courtesy of Christie's South Kensington.)

Fan, the paper leaf painted by Thomas Robins with elegant company visiting Ralph Allen's stone quarry at Prior Park; with ivory sticks. English, c. 1735. 11 in. (Photograph by courtesy of Christie's.)

Right above: English topographical fan, painted with figures before Cliveden House, Taplow, Bucks; the ivory sticks carved and painted. Mid-18th century. 10 in. (Photograph by courtesy of Christie's.)

Right below: Fine fan, the leaf painted with a shepherd and shepherdess; with ivory sticks. Mid-18th century. $10\frac{1}{2}$ in. (Photograph by courtesy of Christie's.)

In England the topographical fan appeared about 1740. Some of these have been identified by John Harris as being by Thomas Robins, including Christie's, 6 November 1972, lot 172 (270 gns.: see illustration), of elegant company visiting Ralph Allen's stone quarry at Prior Park. On this fan the reserves are decorated with a geometrical pattern. Other examples, possibly by Robins, include a view of Belvoir Castle (de Vere Green, colour plate 26). Another example of a topographical fan, a little later, is the bright and colourful view of Covent Garden Market (CSK, Baldwin Coll., 4 May 1978, lot 78, £680); it is rather crudely drawn, but this is typical of many English fans. Another interesting example is (Christie's, 3 May 1972, lot 91, 180 gns: see illustration) the view of Cliveden, possibly by Goupy; and at Wilton House near Salisbury there is a fan painted with a view of the house by Richard Wilson.

In Holland at the time leaves were painted

*Fan, the leaf painted with a wedding dance;
the mother-of-pearl sticks pierced and gilt. French,
c. 1760. (Photograph by courtesy of Christie's:
11 June 1974, lot 19, 240 gns.)*

with pastoral scenes, often very finely drawn, predominately in tones of pale greens and blue (Christie's, 24 November 1969, lot 111, 70 gns: see illustration p. 33). These fans were fairly small but later, about 1760, they span wider (CSK, Baldwin Coll., 4 May 1978, lot 19, £240). In Venice, fans remained large, *à grand vol:* for instance, Christie's, 16 May 1973, lot 44, 180 gns (see illustration opposite).

During the 1760s the shape and design of fans change. Far more fans survive from this period and they are now normally arranged with one large and two smaller vignettes (CSK, Baldwin Coll., 4 May 1978, lot 106, £220: see colour plate opposite). The finest French fans are exquisitely drawn and tend to be more sombre in colour than those of other European countries. The cheaper French fans are usually painted with dumpy figures with round pink faces.

Typical French fan subjects of the time were pretty groups of lovers, sacrifices to Hymen

*Left above: Fan, the leaf painted with pastoral
lovers, the reverse with figures in a landscape; the
mother-of-pearl sticks carved, pierced and gilt.
French, c. 1750. 11 in. (Photograph by courtesy of
Christie's South Kensington.)*

*Left below: Fan, the leaf painted with the gods on
Olympus, the reverse with Jacob at the Well;
the mother-of-pearl sticks carved, pierced, gilt
and backed. Anglo-Venetian, c. 1760. 10 in.
(Photograph by courtesy of Christie's.)*

Right above: Fan, the leaf painted with a pastoral scene; with pierced ivory sticks. Dutch, c. 1760, with Chinese sticks probably imported from England. In the collection of the Hon. C. A. Lennox-Boyd. (Photograph by courtesy of Christie's South Kensington: 18 July 1973, lot 234.)

Right below: Fan, the leaf painted with King David leading the Ark of the Covenant; with chinoiserie pierced and carved ivory sticks. The leaf Italian, the sticks English, c. 1740. 11½ in; in contemporary fan case inscribed Hodgson, Cheapside. (Photograph by courtesy of Christie's South Kensington: 23 October 1979, lot 6, £ 160.)

Marriage fan, the leaf painted with the arrival of a princess to marry a French prince, the reverse with a mansion. The ivory sticks carved, pierced, gilt, backed with mother-of-pearl and painted with portraits of the bridal couple. French, c. 1760; the reverse 19th century. 11¾ in. (Photograph by courtesy of Christie's South Kensington: 23 October 1979, lot 155, £ 820.)

(commemorating marriages), families and shepherdessess. A fine example commemorating the marriage of the Dauphin and Marie Antoinette in 1770 was sold at CSK, 13 July 1978 (lot 146, £360). This fan can be traced back as previously sold at the Hôtel Drouot, Paris, 13 April 1897 (lot 1, as the property of Madame x).

In Holland a similar arrangement of three vignettes is deployed but leaving much more blank background. One finds a series of fans commemorating Zoutman, the Dutch commander at the Dogger Bank in 1781. Most Dutch fans, however, have Biblical and pastoral subjects. Fans were used in church, where respectable women prayed behind their fans, whilst men used their hats. The Biblical fans were mainly of Old Testament subjects, those of the New Testament being considered idolatrous by Calvinists. By the early 19th century the custom of taking fans to church began to die out. Dr van Eeghen, in her article in *The Bridge* (no. 8, 1966),

Fan, the leaf painted with a trompe l'œil of cards, watercolours and pamphlets, signed Ioh Georg Hertel, excud. Aug. V; the ivory sticks carved, pierced, painted and gilt. Augsburg, c. 1760. 11¼ in. (Photograph by courtesy of Christie's South Kensington.)

says that young women took any fan to church, although it is not known if they went as far as Englishwomen of an earlier generation, who took to church fans painted with 'naked Cupids and women almost so', to the horror of *Lady's Magazine* (March 1776).

A fashion for *trompe l'œil* fans emerges in the 1760s. These are painted with a medley of drawings, pictures, playing cards, jewels and lace, lying on a marble table or a silk table-cover, and are often dated and signed, sometimes by Italians and Germans, the signatures normally being disguised by being on one of the paintings. There is an example in the Castle Museum, York. For a German example, see CSK, Baldwin Coll., 4 May 1978, lot 92 (£760: see illustration), and CSK, 17 May 1979, lot 19 for a Dutch example.

Fan, painted with a view of a harbour, the reverse with a view of Vesuvius. Italian, c. 1740. 11 in. (Photograph by courtesy of Christie's.)

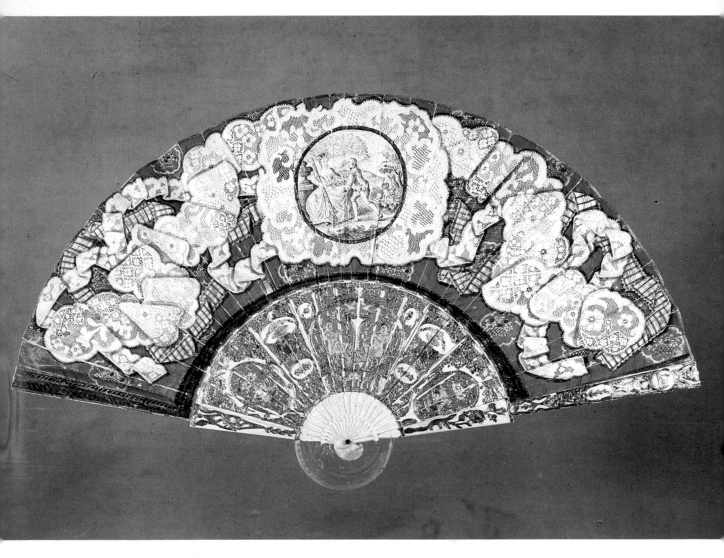

Fan, the chickenskin leaf drawn with a vignette of a gardener presenting a basket of flowers to a sportswoman, on a painted trompe l'œil ground of ribbon lace, the reverse with a trompe l'œil of prints. Possibly Flemish, c. 1770. 11½ in. (Photograph by courtesy of Christie's South Kensington: 23 October 1979, lot 69, £ 340.)

Some appear stylistically to be English. A number of prettier examples with much lace in them are to be found in the Madrid Exhibition of 1920; they were probably French or Italian, made for export to Spain. Late examples of the genre are Assignat fans, with leaves painted or printed with an assortment of bonds used in Revolutionary France. Some *trompe l'œil* fans were also certainly English. Perhaps it is true to say that *trompe l'œil* style is universal. There was a charming earlier Italian example with the *trompe l'œil* used merely as reserves (Christie's, 24 November 1969, lot 106, 85 gns: see illustration opposite).

39

Detail of the handle of a fan, the chickenskin leaf painted with a trompe l'œil of prints against a blue ground; the ivory sticks pierced and carved, with closed-edge carving of flowers, the handle with figures on a bridge. c. 1760, 11½ in. (Photograph by courtesy of Christie's South Kensington.)

fans from this period commemorate balloon ascents; they are very much sought after (CSK, Baldwin Coll., 4 May 1978, lot 119, £820: see illustration on previous page). But from this moment until the Restoration France did not produce many more painted fans. Cheap printed fans with political slogans were popular during revolutionary times. France then, soon after the Revolution, led the field of the finer printed fans at the turn of the century. And as we have seen in Chapter 2, under Napoleon small silk fans, often decorated with spangles, were popular.

In England, the brisé fan returned to favour, longer than those of the early 18th century and still as narrow, often embellished with printed decorations but sometimes with very well painted vignettes (see illustration p. 18; possibly painted by Angelica Kauffmann, R.A.). It is probable that some of these ivory brisé fans were carved in Dieppe: excellent brisé fans were being produced by the

renewed Dieppe industry at that time and an example was presented to Marie Antoinette.

Having broadly covered France, England, Italy and Holland from whence most European fans emanated at the time, it now remains for us to try and sort out Spain, Portugal, Germany, Switzerland and North European and Scandinavian countries such as Sweden.

All fan collectors and enthusiasts are still trying to group fans into countries of origin. It is very hard to do so since, as we have already seen, sticks and leaves were often imported from different countries. What one can do, however, is to pore over old catalogues of exhibitions in the 19th century and early in this century, and catalogues of collections, and work out where most of a certain type were found; it is then probable that they originated there or were commissioned for that country. There was a magnificent exhibition in Madrid in 1920 with 491 exhibits, from which one can judge which types of fans the Spanish favoured.

No. 133, for instance, is a *trompe l'œil* fan with two oval portraits and other pictures strewn amongst playing cards; the Ace is inscribed 'Real Fabris Madrid 1757', but the fan is painted in the French manner. It is therefore probably French for the Spanish market. No. 146 is a printed calendar fan, in Spanish, probably English for the Spanish market.

One has to remember the strong political ties Spain had with both Naples and the Vatican at that time. Exhibits Nos 109 and 110 were two fan leaves lent by the Spanish National Library painted with views of the triumphal square in Naples for Don Carlos Borbón, Infante de España's return from Sicily. They were designed by Francisco de la Vega (a Spaniard), and executed by Cayetana Sardi, Rome. There are two other fans after de la Vega in the Schreiber Collection: entry of Charles, King of the Two Sicilies (Don Carlos Borbón to the Spanish), into Naples (1734), painted by Cayetano Pichini, Rome (s.u. 377), and the review at Gaeta, painted by Leonardo Egiarman, Flamenco ('the Fleming'). They are drawn with a pen in bistre and washed with Indian ink; ornaments are composed of fleur-de-lys similarly drawn on a ground slightly coloured red.

The Spaniards seem to have favoured plenty of portraits and elaborate sticks. In No. 88 in the Madrid Exhibition, the leaf is printed with lovers and two miniatures of a couple and the tops of the sticks are carved with beautiful portraits, probably five versions of the same couple (c. 1760; from the collection of Queen Victoria Eugenia of Spain). The sticks of No. 159 are set with eighteen portrait miniatures.

No. 67 in the exhibition is an unusual fan with carved and pierced serpentine sticks; the painted leaf, depicting Alexander the Great, has scalloped edges rather like webbed feet. It dates from about 1770.

No. 75 has sticks with two Chinese figures in the handle (like the fan in the plate on page 42); the sides of the sticks are elaborately carved like a fore-edge painting in relief (or should one say a side-edge painting?). No. 129 is similarly carved with figures at a window. This type of fan is thought by Peter Thornton to be Portuguese. He describes one in the Victoria and Albert Museum carved with a garland of flowers round the closed sticks.

Fan, the leaf with a hand-coloured etching of the Plaza Mayor, Madrid, embellished with a procession, the reserves painted with putti and banners, inscribed Viva Carlos IIII and Viva el Principe y la Princesa, the reverse painted with a bullfight; the tortoiseshell sticks carved, pierced and gilt. Spanish, probably c. 1788. 11 in. (Photograph by courtesy of Christie's South Kensington.)

Fan, the leaf painted with a game of blind man's buff watched by Harlequin; the ivory sticks painted with fruit, pierced and gilt. 9 in. In the collection of the Hon. C. A. Lennox-Boyd. (Photograph by courtesy of Christie's South Kensington: from the remaining contents of 22 Kensington Palace Gardens, London, W8, sold by the family of the Duquesa de Marchena, 12 December 1977, lot 111.)

No. 8 in the same exhibition (c. 1740; lent by Queen Christina of Spain) has remarkably straight guardsticks – perhaps this is a Spanish trait. When folded up they look like a box.

No. 34 (c. 1760) has very elaborate carved and pierced mother-of-pearl sticks containing painted lacquered cartouches (like the superb but damaged fan CSK, 23 October 1979, lot 82, £150).

Topographical fans are always fun. No. 117 in the Madrid Exhibition was painted by a hack fan painter, probably Spanish, with the market in the Plaza de la Cebada, Madrid; the reverse has the Plaza Mayor (c. 1760).

The fan was from the collection of the Duke of Alba. The sticks were painted with scallop shells and butterflies, which seems very Spanish in taste. No. 123 shows the Plaza Mayor in 1765 (CSK, Baldwin Coll., 4 May 1978, lot 101, £350: see illustration on previous page – a similar view, but a hand-coloured etching). No. 100 is painted with a bullfight in the same Plaza (c. 1760), with what appears to be an architect in the foreground; from the collection of the Infanta Doña Isabel.

Lace often appears in *trompe l'œil* fans: see No. 96 in the Madrid Exhibition (coll. Queen Christina of Spain) – a particularly charming mid-18th-century example with yards of lace loosely unfurled right across the leaf. A similar example was sold at CSK, 17 May 1979 (lot 75, £260). In No. 130 the lace theme also appears in the sticks, and in No. 192 the lace meanders like a path between lunettes.

Very much to the Spanish taste seem *trompe l'œil* fans with irregular-shaped vignettes, often in monochrome. No. 89 is an example; this has the wide-spanning *battoire* sticks favoured by the Spaniards. No. 118 in the same exhibition is another example (c. 1740); the irregular-shaped vignettes are echoed in the sticks.

No. 191 in the Madrid Exhibition is a beautiful example of a mica chinoiserie fan. The leaf appears to be mica painted wih a bamboo palisade, birds and flowers. Three European portrait miniatures hang in the centre above a chinoiserie couple at tea (c. 1760); this fan was from the collection of the Duquesa de Fernán Núñez. No. 158 is a very elaborate fan, decorated with a staircase and arch of straw-work, in a style usually associated with France, but the painting looks very Spanish.

There are some neo-classical fans but again, many appear to be of Italian or English origin.

Although it appears that very few fans were produced in Spain in the 18th century, they were in fact regarded with very high esteem in the peninsula and the Spanish nobility ordered a large number of fans from France, England and Italy at that time. I feel that many of the important fan commissions were very precise orders, as the fans from Spain tend to be, on the whole, a little more elaborate and more flashy than those found elsewhere. One can only assume that the fan-makers produced a certain number of fans with the Spanish market in mind. Until more research has been pursued it is impossible to be more definitive. Certainly the high regard for fans in Spain must have led to the safe keeping of such fine examples.

Fan, the leaf painted with fashionable company at tea, the reverse with a bunch of flowers; the ivory sticks carved and pierced. German, probably Nuremberg, c. 1735. 11 in. (Photograph by courtesy of Christie's South Kensington.)

Fan, the leaf painted with musique champêtre after Watteau; the ivory sticks painted with shells. Probably South German, c. 1730. (Photograph by courtesy of Christie's South Kensington: 17 May 1979, lot 65, £140.)

Under Spanish fans, I feel one must include all the French, English and Italian fans designed for the Spanish market. The more one looks at reference books such as the Madrid Exhibition catalogues, the more one can gauge Spanish taste in fans in the 18th century. Their taste is very elaborate but it seems catered for almost entirely by imports, except for the topographical fans. Some of the fans painted with bright earth colours and purple may be German (CSK, Baldwin Coll., 4 May 1978, lot 86, £840: see p. 45); they often have elaborate sticks. Some of the fans of net (c. 1760) applied with painted vignettes are also thought to be German. It is possible that the fans decorated with elaborate straw-work are German (Christie's, 27 February 1972, lot 171: see illustration p. 16), also possibly fans with articulated sticks, where they are not French. On the other hand, Anna-liese Ohm in her 1972 article felt that no German fan industry existed in the 18th century.

No. 47 in the Karlsruhe Exhibition is a watercolour fan leaf of 'Winter' by Johan Holzer (1708–40). It is from a set of four, and this artist is also known to have painted another set of four fan leaves. The German fan painters may have been the *Hausmäler*

who decorated china from the princely factories. A fan by a Meissen painter, J. C. Hahnemann, is illustrated in R. Haehl's biography of Samuel Hahnemann (Leipzig 1822). The younger Hahnemann was a famous doctor, the father of homoeopathy. In the exhibition *Fans from the East* (plate 32) there was a strange fan from an Austrian museum painted with a chinoiserie design reminiscent of blanc-de-Chine figures and the work of Pillement, and dating from about 1760.

So far, the only fans known to have come from Switzerland are a charming group by Johannes Sulzer, 'au Rossignol à Win-

One of a pair of fans painted with scenes from country life and decorated with straw-work cages; with ivory sticks. By Johannes Sulzer, Swiss, c. 1780. 11 in. (Photograph by courtesy of Christie's.)

terthur' (1748–94). They are mainly signed and he also notes that he both painted and mounted them; so it must have been a small factory. There were three in the Karlsruhe Exhibition (No. 61). They are delicately painted with small pastoral vignettes and decorated with spy holes in the form of objects such as bird cages. Three were sold at Christie's 27 May 1970 (lot 251, 140 gns; see illustration on previous page); Christie's also sold a similar fan in the sale of 12 March 1973 (lot 91, 38 gns, unsigned). There are twelve others in Swiss museums (see the Fan Circle, bulletin No. 11). Christie's also sold an interesting series of Swiss designs for fans (18 July 1973, lot 225, £180), figures in fancy dress at a musical evening, some inscribed 'de Flummeren… St. Gallens… orn… 1775'. (In January 1980 CSK sold other fans with Swiss views, c. 1780.)

In Sweden, Crown Princess Louisa Ulrike instituted the Order of the Fan in 1744. Britta Hammar has established that fans were certainly made in Sweden in the 18th century; the fanmakers registered their marks with local councils and she lists a number of Swedish fanmakers from the 1770s. Kulturen Museum possesses one hallmarked Stockholm 1765 and so is able to tie it to one of four fanmakers who submitted fans that year. Apparently, it compares with the simpler imported articles – Miss Hammar also notes an interesting comparison:

Carl Tersmeden in his memoirs writes that he bought two beautiful fans at the Hedemora fair for his sisters at 15 platar each. In the same year he rented two beautifully furnished rooms and attic in a house near the castle in the old town of Gamla Stan for 12 platar a month.

Who were the fan painters? Hardly any signed their work before the last decades of the 19th century. Some, of course, were good and will eventually be identified. The brisé painters were often trained as miniaturists, but the paper and silk painters were not, and if they did double as decorative painters, it was in a trade as anonymous as fan painting. A few hands, like that of the damaged fan, CSK, 23 October 1979, are distinctive. An English or Anglo-Italian painter of the 1770s who used curiously shaped vignettes, known from two fans (one illustrated in colour plate opposite), is almost identifiable, as two similarly shaped drawings by him survive, with inscriptions, dates and signatures, the last unfortunately and tantalizingly just cut off. The painter of CSK, Baldwin Coll., 4 May 1978, lot 89 (£280), composed his leaf in a different way and was probably the painter of CSK, 17 May 1979, lot 56.

With a few Italian painters we know their names, for they signed their fans or designs. Unfortunately, we know not much more. If they are recorded, it is a brief note in Pascoli's *Vita di' Pittori* of 1730 or other such book.

At least two Roman firms, 'Camill' Butin' of 1800 (Christie's, 21 November 1972, lot 200) and Leonardo Germo, signed their works, as did Sulzer of Winterthur. A small set of fan leaves survive, one apparently signed 'Pietro Fabris'. Four fans in the Chinese manner, said to have been painted by Fr Castiglione at the court of Qianlong in Peking, were exhibited in New York in 1938. No French fan painter signed his work, although many people signed fans 'Boucher' and 'Watteau'. Watteau drew Pierrot on a paper fan leaf but did not make a habit of it. Two or three other such drawings probably exist. (See E. Croft-Murray, 'Watteau's design for a fan leaf', *Apollo,* March 1974.)

In England and the Netherlands a bit more is known about fan painters. Thomas Robins the elder painted at least two fans; he was a flower painter and garden designer and among his sketch books, still belonging to his family, is a design for one. Another painter, Joseph Goupy (fl. 1711 on; d. 1763), is traditionally said to have done fan leaves,

Fan, the paper leaf with a curiously-shaped classical vignette within a reserve of peacock feathers on sprigs and swags of flowers, the ivory sticks pierced, the guardsticks backed with pink tinsel. c. 1770. 11¼ in. (Photograph by courtesy of Christie's: 17 July 1972, lot 135, £ 35.)

but until a design or a documented fan emerges, we can but guess at his work. He was appointed cabinet painter to Frederick, Prince of Wales, and is most likely to have painted the fan of Cliveden (see illustration p. 33), where his patron lived. A third English fan painter was Antonio Poggi, a Corsican, who appears to have been a protégé of Reynolds. He published printed fans by Bartolozzi after Kauffmann, and organized an exhibition of fan designs at Christie's in 1782. One of these designs, Angelica Kauffmann's 'Three Graces', reappeared there in 1971 (9 November, lot 96, £1,050: see illustration); it has been much copied, as it was the basis for one of Bartolozzi's prints. For the rest of the 18th century, fan painters are anonymous figures. Many may have had other artistic work. Only one painter showed the slightest similarity in composition to contemporary illustrators and only a handful of other fans are drawn in a similar way. The reverses of many fans show charming free brush work such as appears on Delft and Lowestoft pottery of the same period. Francis Simbert, a pupil of Kneller who practised in Boston, Mass., used to import fans in large quantities; these were probably plain, and he or a fellow artist could have painted the design wanted. Amateurs abound: the painter of lot 37, CSK, 17 May 1979, was probably an amateur who had learnt to draw in the 1770s at Cambridge, where a school of caricaturists had grown up.

As for Dutch fans, Dr van Eeghen has catalogued the designs of 'Miss' Johanna Alethea Oosterdijk (1736–1813), the daughter of a professor in Utrecht. Among the handful of Dutch fan painters who signed their work is a distinguished classical painter, Frans Xavery, who died in 1768, the last of his line. He signed two excellent fans in Dr van Eeghen's collection; one painted with the Queen of Sheba is also inscribed 'inv:et' meaning that Xavery had designed the fan, the other, the Altar of Love, is inscribed 'fecit' on a log, and dated 1762, meaning that he painted it but did not design it.

Another Dutch fan painter who signed his work was Johannes Van Dregt (1737–1807). The well-known watercolour painter Dirk Langendijk (1748–1805) is known from one fan, a commission from a print for the silver wedding anniversary of a friend in Rotterdam. A Dutch amateur, Lt. d'Art [Lieutenant in the Artillery] van Barenburg, a member of a family of soldiers, signed his *trompe l'œil* fan; he would have learnt drawing as part of his gunnery training. Apart from these, Dutch fan painters are anonymous.

The professionals worked either in the makers' workshops in the cities or at home; one can presume that the better work was done in workshops, often by more than one painter. In Holland, Dr van Eeghen has pointed out that each workshop had its trademark – e.g. two sections of green fence, or one iron gate and a single green fence: probably Amsterdam – which was incorporated into the design of the vignette on the reverse of the fan. The other painters were probably provincial hacks, possibly journeymen engravers, china painters, coach painters and local drawing masters of whom we would know nothing anyway. It might be tempting to attribute examples to distinguished local decorators but the fan trade is too widespread. It is quite possible, for example, that Beilby, the Newcastle glass painter, painted fans for his family, but they could be given to relations elsewhere and so disappear into the wide world. The Meis-

sen painter J.C.Hahnemann painted a fan for his daughter-in-law, but it was his son Samuel's fame as a doctor that led to its survival with its provenance.

In hardly any other European countries are fans signed. The Swedish-born Danish Court painter Carl Gustaf Pilo (1711–93) signed one in 1740 and a Flemish amateur, C. de Stirum, whose family is still well known in Belgium, signed a charming fan in 1792.

Did famous artists paint fans for patrons in the 18th century? It is unlikely, as the greatest artists had studios and some assistant could have painted them, and a lesser artist would have been too insistent on his own status to do this: he could have painted a fan for an equal but not for a superior, and if his patron were his equal he would not have painted a fan. But as yet not enough is known to refute the idea completely, and, after all, all famous artists are not rich and famous all their lives.

However, artists skilled in water- and bodycolour painting may have done fans for their relations, and when faced with old age may have turned their brush to a fan. Richard Wilson, the impecunious but greatest landscape painter of the 18th century, is known to have designed, if not painted, a pole screen.

But if the leaves and fans travelled, so did the painters. The Flemish fan painters, with their distinctive colouring of muted purple and tight drawing, probably worked in France and in England. A group of Italians, mainly Venetian or Venetian-inspired, worked in London in the second half of the century. Their training had included 'composition' which English painters had not mastered – had, in fact, not needed to master, as very little decorative painting was done before 1750. Their leaders were G.B.Cipriani and Angelica Kauffmann, but their followers were many and some leaves may also have been painted in Italy especially for the tourist market.

51

Fan, the leaf a hand-coloured etching of a scene at the Fountain of Love, a lady being presented with a flower by her lover, and another lady being serenaded and brought a letter by a dog, the reverse with the words of a song, 'La Fontaine de l'Amour'; on wooden sticks. French, c. 1780. $10\frac{3}{4}$ in. (Photograph by courtesy of Christie's South Kensington.)

Right: Masquerade fan, the leaf a hand-coloured etching of a face, with two vignettes from life, a fan shop and a music shop; the ivory sticks painted with flowers. English for the Spanish market, c. 1740. $10\frac{1}{2}$ in. (Photograph by courtesy of Christie's South Kensington.)

4

Printed Fans

In about the 1720s, the fanmakers, despite their enormous success at the top of the market, found it necessary to expand their trade and produce cheaper fans in bulk to appease an ever-increasing public demand. In order to do so, they began printing the leaves – they could then duplicate their designs and their products could be sold cheaply at fairs on stalls and at booths, thus undercutting the cheap Chinese fans that were swamping the market at the lower end: the dilemma is very well explained in the chapter on chinoiserie in *Fans from the East*. Printed fans are used to commemorate events such as balloon ascents. They would have been taken home as souvenirs, and obviously sold by the thousand. Being cheap and ephemeral at the time they were often not kept – unlike fans of the highest quality made from precious materials; their sticks are often only of plain wood. As many of these printed fans are rare, their value often rivals in price other important fans. For instance, whereas the rare mica fan of about 1700, lot 100 in the Baldwin Collection, realized £2,600 at CSK (see illustration p. 21), the printed mask fan, c. 1740, lot 18 in the same sale on 4 May 1978 realized £2,100 (see colour plate). As we shall see later on in this book, other examples of this charming fan exist, together with a water-colour version in the Metropolitan Museum of Art; in the painted version there are slight variations; for instance, there are fewer masquerade fans on the counter than in the prin-

ted version and the two lower scenes are transposed.

The fan printers took advantage of the 1734 Copyright Act, which proved to be of great assistance not only to them but also to fan collectors and historians later – just as hall-marking has proved invaluable to collectors of silver. English printed fans after 1734 may have the name of the publisher, often his or her address and the date of publication; sadly, as this was usually at the foot of the leaf, it has often been snipped or guillotined during mounting, but as long as one copy survives with the publication line all fans from that plate can be dated. Of course, publishers were not obliged by law to copyright their designs. This would be another reason for no publisher's name appearing on a printed fan. Another amusing point: some dates,

names and initials are sometimes disguised in the body of the design, as they occasionally are in painted fans, particularly *trompe l'œil* fans.

The most important and comprehensive collection of printed fans is that formed by Lady Charlotte Schreiber and presented to the British Museum in 1891 by her. It is a fantastic collection of some 734 fans, both mounted and unmounted, of which only about 100 are painted. Most of the printed fans are English – nearly 300; just over 200 are French; the rest are divided more or less as follows: German 23, Italian 18, Spanish 17, 'Dutch' 3, Japanese 1, American 1. As Lady Charlotte was English, it is natural that she should collect mainly English fans but she was widely travelled and her collection probably provided a good ratio of the sources of printed fans. In the 18th century, England seems to have led the market and exported fans in quantity, sometimes suitably translated versions. Madame de Pompadour in 1760 asks her brother to provide her with printed English fans for presents – not so pretty but cheaper than those that could be obtained elsewhere; see Nancy Mitford, *Madame de Pompadour*.

Certainly some fans have appeared on the market in the last twelve years that are not to be found in the Schreiber Collection, and there are two or three fine private collections of printed fans, but rarely have more than two or three examples of each fan, if that, been seen in the saleroom during the last decade. This must prove that printed fans are comparatively rare, except perhaps those lithographic fans of the mid-19th century. However, one collector has recently made a remarkable find. He bought bundles of unmounted fan leaves from an old print dealer consisting of both Peninsular War propaganda fans printed in Spanish and theatrical designs; a high proportion are designs in Lady Charlotte's collection and he feels certain he has tapped one of her sources.

Etching

Most of the 18th-century English and European printed fans are etchings, the simplest reproductive method of the period, often coloured later by hand. Etching is the method whereby the pattern in the metal plate is made by acid biting away the metal where a protective wax has been scratched away. It is the cheapest method and the most commercial; the artist works straight on to the copper plate. It produces an effect not unlike an India ink drawing or the finest brushwork of a Chinese painting, and it sometimes requires more than a good magnifying glass to tell the difference.

English 18th-century printed fans cover a wide range of subjects. Lionel Cust in his catalogue of Lady Charlotte Schreiber's collection divided them into nine subsections: Portraits, Historical, The Peninsular War, Classical and Biblical, Fancy, Social, Pastoral, Literature, Painting, etc., Theatrical, Instructive and Amusing. These headings give an immediate idea of the range of subjects covered.

Printed fans often bear titles. These include 'A New Game of Piquet now in play among Different Nations in Europe' in English (S.M.1, U.M.); another example of this fan, in French, was sold at CSK in the Baldwin Collection (lot 21, £490: see illustration opposite). The ten female figures representing France, Spain, Sardinia, Austria, Saxony, Russia, Poland, Britannia, Holland and Prussia are seated round a table with all except the last three taking hands in a game of piquet, Pope Innocent XI declining to take part although his chair is at the ready; on the right stands a commentator and on the extreme right are the Sultan of Turkey and the Shah of Persia. This fan alludes to the intrigues of European diplomacy concerning the affairs of Poland. Madeleine Ginsburg of the Victoria and Albert Museum informs me that an unmounted leaf in the Cabinet des Estam-

pes, Bibliothèque Nationale, is dated in another hand 'October 4th, 1733', when the French entered the war of the Polish Succession, before the Partition. About ten copies of this fan are known.

Other historical fans in the Schreiber Collection include one depicting the Coronation Banquet of George II, 11 October 1727 (S.M.2 and S.U.), with the Champion of England challenging the guests. Sir Robert Strange, the Jacobite, engraved a fan (S.M. 3) as a memorial to the Jacobite rebellion in 1745 with Prince Charles Edward Stuart in armour attended by Cameron of Lochiel as Mars and Flora Macdonald as Bellona;

like many classical scenes, it is rich in allegory. On 14 July 1969 Christie's sold a more straightforward version of another incident in the rebellion (Bompas Coll., lot 74, 32 gns). Another fan, 'View of the Trial of Warren Hastings, Esq., at Westminster Hall published by Cock & Co., 36 Snow Hill, 22 Sept. 1788' (S.M.7 and S.U.31), was obviously so successful as the trial went on so long and was of interest to tourists, that it was translated for foreigners (see Bompas Coll., 14 July 1969, lot 77, 28 gns, where a Spanish translation has been stuck over the English version), who looked upon the trial as the pursuit of a corrupt public servant rather

Printed fan, Jeu de Piquet des Différentes Nations de l'Europe, hand-coloured etching; with pierced ivory sticks. 10¾ in. (Photograph by courtesy of Christie's South Kensington.)

Printed fan, the mount a hand-coloured etching by Gyles King of an allegory on the marriage of Princess Anne with the Prince of Orange (1734), showing the bride and bridegroom, Hymen, angels and putti in a landscape, with a building and ships in the background; with pierced ivory sticks, the handle forming a heart. c. 1734. 10¾ in.; sticks damaged. (Photograph by courtesy of Christie's.)

than a witch-hunt conducted by a bunch of ignorant and bigoted Whigs. There is one ballooning fan with Messrs. Charles and Robert's Balloon (1783) and Biagini's Air Balloon and an accident, although most of the surviving ballooning fans are French. Other subjects included the temporary buildings erected in Green Park for the splendid firework display of 27 April 1749, to celebrate the Peace of Aix-la-Chapelle (s.m. 4). Unfortunately the fan was published on 7 October 1748, and missed all the drama when the grand setpiece caught fire prematurely, and the grand finale with the chief engineer being set about with his walk-

56

ing stick by the German who had designed the display.

As the reign of George III covers most of the period there are, of course, a number of fans alluding to him which were suitable for export both to Hanover and to any country which Great Britain was allied at the time. These include 'Vive le Roy', engraved by Simpkins and published by T. T. Balster, 19 March 1789 (S.M. 9); another example was sold at Christie's (Bompas Coll., 14 July 1969, lot 72, 15 gns); and 'The Royal Family at the Exhibition of the Royal Academy' (S.U. 34), published by Antonio Poggi, 6 March 1789. It is interesting to note that this fan leaf, engraved by P. Martini after H. Ramberg, is taken from Martini's original plate, the print having been cut down to the shape of a fan. Poggi, a protégé of Reynolds, sold a collection of a hundred of his designs at Christie's on 29 March 1783; he even persuaded the great Bartolozzi to engrave fans for him. Other patriotic fans include George III and Queen Charlotte (S.M. 9).

Amongst the earliest English topical fans is a satire on Sir Robert Walpole's hated Excise Bill (1733), which reminds Walpole that it was a similar bill that helped to bring down Cardinal Wolsey. Walpole took the hint and withdrew the bill. There was a sequel, 'The Motion', engraved by H. Franks and published 6 February 1741 (S.U. 22 and 23).

The marriage of Princess Anne, daughter of George II, with William, Prince of Orange, on 14 March 1734, produced a flow of fans for the English and Dutch markets, many of them highly allegorical, strewn with orange trees (S.U. 24, 25, 26, 27 and 28 and S.M. 325); Christie's sold yet another version (28 July 1971, lot 32, 38 gns: see illustration opposite), engraved by Gyles King and showing the couple attended by Hymen, angels and putti, and in the foreground the verse: 'The Gods in Consult does Agree... Orange triumphant is again'. The ivory

handle closes to form a heart. Madeleine Ginsburg tells me that advertisements by Gamble and Pinchbeck for Royal wedding fans of various types appear in newspapers as early as 1733.

Military matters remember among other subjects the triumphs of Frederick the Great in 'Veni, Vidi, Vici', an English export fan, probably produced in about 1761 as it is an allegory of his triumphs in the Seven Years' War (CSK, Baldwin Coll., 4 May 1978, lot 36, £240); 'The Capture of Portobello', published by F. Chassereau, 22 April 1740 (S.U. 29); 'The Attack on Cartagena', also by Admiral Vernon (S.U. 30); and 'Nelson and Victory', 1798 (S.M. 15) – this last also lists '18 New Country Dances for 1799' and was sold by 'Principal Haberdashers in London'.

Amongst portraits there are royal portraits, a fan portraying Sir Thomas White, founder of St John's College, Oxford, adapted from the Oxford Almanack for 1733 (S.U. 19 and S.E. 4) and the 'Camperdown Fan, or the Glorious 11th October 1797', published 10 March 1798 by Reben, 42 Pall Mall (Christie's, 27 May 1970, lot 199, 22 gns).

Biblical subjects on printed fans again date mainly from the mid-18th century and are therefore etchings. There are comparatively few of them, as these subjects appear to have been reserved for the more expensive market, painted fans. They include 'Moses Striking the Rock', published by M. Gamble, 1740 (S.M. 20); 'The Birth of Esau and Jacob' (S.M. 19 and S.E. 126); and 'St Paul Preaching at Athens' (S.M. 21). These would mainly have been used as church fans.

There is also a small group of classical fans, e.g. Telemachus and Mentor landing on the island of Calypso (S.M. 25); Diana and Nymphs (S.M. 22); but there is a larger group, mainly stipple engravings, at the end of the 18th century.

The social printed fans are often particularly entertaining. These include 'Mr. Thomas Osbourne's Duck-Hunting', 1754 (S.M. 40,

*Loterie de l' Amour, a hand-coloured etching by Couturbier; with
wooden sticks with an ivory dial in the guardstick. French, c. 1775. In the
collection of the Hon. C. A. Lennox-Boyd.*

S.E. 123 and 124). Osbourne was a publisher
and bookseller. On 10 September 1754 he
gave a house-warming breakfast with dancing and band in the marquee and duck-
shooting for the gentlemen at his new
Hampstead home. The 'New Opera Fan for
1797' is a seating plan with names of the
occupants of boxes, published by W.Cock
(S.M. 62 and S.E. 142); the King's Theatre
fan (1788) has the Prince of Wales and Mrs
Fitzherbert in box 63 (S.M. 43 and S.E. 128).
There are also fans describing how to play
games and to dance the latest dances, such
as the Casino fan (1793) (S.M. 49 and
S.E. 130), published by Sarah Ashton, and

Dance fans for 1792, 1793 and 1794 (S.M.
48, 50 and 51 and S.E. 131 and 134) by various publishers. The Royal Connection fan
gives the rules of Connection, a card game
invented by H.R.H. Princess Elizabeth and
the Duchess of York; it was published by
Seckars, Scott and Grosky of Friday St.
Then there are various tourist and souvenir
fans for fashionable places; Ranelagh (S.U.
105 and S.E. 51); the Pump Room at Bath
(S.U. 106 and S.E. 46), published by G.Speren
1737; the Crescent at Buxton (S.U. 108 and
S.E. 67); at Christie's, 30 July 1974 (lot 175,
70 gns) was the Margate fan, or Guide to
the Isle of Thanet, the reverse with a map
of Thanet and a directory, published by
W.Else (1805). The New Camp Fan of 1794
(S.M. 52 and S.E. 135; there is another of the
same in Worthing Museum) depicts plans
of camps where the militia is being organized in manoeuvres, and advertises itself
as being 'sold at all the Fan Shops in
London'. Others show 'the Telegraph

recently erected above the Admiralty' (Christie's, 14 July 1969, lot 75; and another example, CSK, 17 May 1979, lot 106).

Other fans were pure entertainment, such as the various Charade fans including 'The New Pick-Nick Charade Fan for the Year 1803' (S.M. 68 and S.E. 158); the 'New Moralist or Way to Wealth' (Christie's, 14 July 1969, lot 69, 40 gns); 'The Wheel of Fortune', engraved by J.Fleetwood, 48 Fetter Lane, in mixed media, stipple and etching (S.M. 65 and S.E. 155; Christie's, 16 May 1973, lot 20 (with another fan), 22 gns). 'The Oracle' (S.M. 65 and S.E. 150, 151), published by Ino. Cock, I.P.Crowder & Co., 21 Wood Street, Cheapside (1800) was a horoscope fan. There is a version in French in the Messel Collection complete with arrow-shaped ivory pointer; another French version, the verse printed on silk with painted putti and gilt ivory sticks, was sold together with an engraved leaf of instructions (CSK, Baldwin Coll., 4 May 1978, lot

81, £480). Both 'Fanology, or the Ladies Conversation Fan' (S.M. 63 and S.E. 147 and 148), designed by Charles Francis Badini, and published by Robert Clarke, 26 Strand, in 1797, and the 'Ladies' Bill of Fare' (S.U. 114 and S.E. 77) were mixed-media fans, line engraving with stipple, the latter with humorous medallions of men as various kinds of lovers, published by G.Wilson, 14 February 1795, 108 St. Martin's Lane, presumably as a Valentine; also in mixed media was 'A selection of Beaux' (S.U. 113 and S.E. 76) (1795).

Then there is a group of more useful and educational fans including a fan listing the

The Art of Divination, a hand-coloured etching of thirty-six ideas, published by Dyde & Scribe, Pall Mall; with wooden sticks. English, c. 1780. 11 in. Not in the Schreiber Collection. (Photograph by courtesy of Christie's South Kensington: 17 May 1979, lot 138, £ 150.)

fares of Hackney coaches (Christie's, 14 July 1969, lot 76, 32 gns); a Botanical Fan (CSK, 17 May 1979, lot 107) (S.U. 195 and S.E. 69 and 70); a History of England since the Conquest (S.M. 72 and S.E. 132 and 133), published by J.Cock and J.P.Crowder (1793) and engraved by S.J.Neele, 352 Strand: the Castle Museum, York has an example of this fan, and there is a similar fan with the History of France (S.M. 73). Particularly useful is the Heraldic Fan (S.U. 198), engraved with a series of heraldic symbols with their denominations published by F.Martin (1792), engraved by Ovenden, sold by Wm. Cook, Fanmaker to the Duchess of York, 50 Pall Mall and 55 St. Paul's Church Yard.

There are so many English pastoral and chinoiserie etched fans that only two need be cited: Christie's, 24 February 1971, lot 10, is a parasol fan, the mount a hand-coloured etching of scenes from rural life, with wooden handle, 12 in. diameter (c. 1750); and a fan etched with a musical party with four printed songs and the reverse with a *trompe l'œil* of prints and lace, with sandalwood sticks, engraved by J.Preston (1781) (Christie's, 3 May 1972, lot 80, 28 gns). Many others have been sold in recent years. Twenty-four are listed in the Schreiber catalogue and a number were exhibited in the *Fans from the East* Exhibition. They are normally pretty but slight.

These fans form the biggest section of general English printed fans, the overall design being intended for colouring, with all details except the clouds lightly etched in. As they are not ephemeral large stocks do not survive: the fans remained in print and saleable for many years. These fans are traditionally dated to the 1740s and 1750s, and the style and technique of the undated ones confirms this. We cannot, however, date the fans themselves so accurately from this, for a coloured fan leaf in the Schreiber Collection has the inscription in the margin 'Mr. M. pattern 1812' – presumably the date when Mr M., whoever he may be, ordered

a new stock of his cheapest fans. One has then to date the colour of the paints or the shape of the sticks.

Another large group consists of small groups of figures, sometimes theatrical, in etched outline; these are printed sometimes from curiously shaped copper plates. Sometimes different examples exist from the same copper plate with one or more figures removed. It is not known whether these copper plates were made for some other purpose, then cut down and the background details removed, or just made on odd bits of copper. When used on a fan the figures are coloured in and very often two buildings are painted on either side, like a castle or an abbey – usually Kirkstall. This method saves the printseller the expense of employing a figure painter. The general crudity and weakness of the painting should not put the collector off any of these etched fans, as they were often issued very crudely coloured. Many mourning fans were made by that method, presumably to be distributed to ladies at funerals.

S.U. 201 is a design for a fan from the *Hibernia Magazine*. This was a folded insert, like the designs for embroidery one finds in the *Ladies' Magazine* (1763 onwards).

A number of etched French fans exist, such as the six designs for fans and a title-page advertisement by Nicholas Loire (1624–79) (S.U. 257–263 and S.F.I) of Biblical and classical subjects: Isaac and Rebecca, The Finding of Moses, Venus, The Judgment of Paris, Europa, and an Eastern goddess. There are also some by Abraham Bosse (1602–76); Marc Rosenberg illustrates a 1638 fan leaf by Bosse, from the collection of G.J.Rosenberg of Karlsruhe, in his foreword to the catalogue of the 1891 Karlsruhe Exhibition. Later French etched fans include a pair of mid-18th-century handscreens applied with hand-coloured etchings of the Châteaux of Versailles and Marly, published by Lattre, rue de Jacques, Bordeaux, and sold together with two other fans at Christie's, 5

One of a pair of printed handscreens applied with hand-coloured etchings of the Châteaux of Versailles and Marly, published by Lattre, rue de St Jacques, Bordeaux. In the collection of the Hon. C. A. Lennox-Boyd. (Photograph by courtesy of Christie's.)

Malbrouk, the leaf with three hand-coloured etched vignettes of the departure, tomb and widow of the Duke of Marlborough, the reverse with the words and music of 'La Mort de Mr. d' Malbrouk'; with wooden sticks. French, c. 1775. 11 in. (Photograph by courtesy of Christie's South Kensington.)

November 1974 (lot 36, 45 gns: see colour plate on previous page). Dr van Eeghen has a pair illustrating the story of Jeannot, published by Md. Petit, rue du Petit Pont Notre Dame. There are several fans lampooning 'Malbrouck', the Duke of Marlborough (s.m. 199–201 and s.u. 38; also csk, 23 October 1979, lot 30, £130: see colour plate). Others include 'Alzianne ou le Pouvoir de l'Amour' (c. 1770) (Christie's 24 February 1971, lot 18); 'Le Triomphe de l'Amour' (s.m. 152; and Christie's, 27 May 1970, lot 249, 7 gns); and Heloise and Abelard (csk, 15 July 1975, lot 169). At the end of the 18th century quite a number of historical and

political fans were produced, these being troubled times: a satirical one, England and America (1778) (s.m. 80 and s.f. 11); the Birth of the Dauphin (1781) (s.m. 82 and s.f. 14); l'Assemblée des Notables (1787) (s.m. 84 and s.f. 27); Louis xvi and Necker (s.m. 87 and s.f. 35); Les Etats Généraux (1789) (s.m. 88 and s.f. 40); The Taking of the Bastille (1789) (s.m. 93 and 41, and several other versions); Assignats (s.m. 116 and s.f. 74: a medley of assignats); Costumes of the Revolution (s.m. 128 and s.f. 71 and 72: fifteen figures dressed in the official robes of the revolutionary government); An Allegory of Bonaparte and the Peace of Amiens (csk, Baldwin Coll., 4 May 1978, lot 46, £170). The colours of French printed fans are often more acid and are often cruder than their English contemporaries. There are also several ballooning fans including the ascent of MM Charles and Robert (1783) (s.m. 138 and s.f. 20), cabriolet fans and fans with scenes from plays.

There are a few Italian etched fans including seven in the Schreiber Collection (S.U. 275, etc.), mainly classical, published by Appo. Pagni, e Bardi in Via Maggio, Firenze, two of them engraved by Carlo Lasinio in 1796, one (Cupid and Psyche) copied from a Bartolozzi fan leaf (S.U. 74), or an almost identical Poggi fan leaf (S.U. 75), both of which were published on 14 August 1795. Cust in his catalogue presumes it is copied from Bartolozzi, who was a Florentine, but C.A.Lennox-Boyd has pointed out to me that Poggi went to Florence to become a picture dealer. Thus, we have English and Italian fans that are almost identical. They vary only in the smallest details – a Cupid here, a caryatid there. With the three fan leaves in the Schreiber Collection there is a slight difference of size, the Florentine fan being slightly smaller.

Occasionally tourist views are found, such as Christie's, 12 March 1973, lot 76, with an oiled paper leaf bearing a hand-coloured etching of St. Peter's, Rome, and ebony sticks ($9\frac{1}{2}$ in., early 19th century).

There are three early Italian fan designs in the Schreiber Collection. 'Battaglia del Re Tessi e del Re Tinta' (S.U. 269 and S.F. 106) is an engraving of a handscreen with a representation of the tournament between the companies of weavers and dyers on the Arno (1619), signed 'Chez N.Bonnart, Jacomo Callot', an early 18th-century copy of an etching by Jacques Callot (1592–1635) (S.U. 27). Another (S.U. 270 and S.F. 108) is a French copy by Nicolas Cochin of an etching by Stefano de la Bella (1610–64), of country dancers. The earliest fan design in

Grammaire Française à l'usage des Rentiers, a hand-coloured etching ; with wooden sticks. Possibly English for the French market, c. 1785. 10 in. In the collection of the Hon. C.A.Lennox-Boyd.

the Schreiber Collection (S.U. 272) is one for a feathered handscreen with variant designs for decorative medallions, by Agostino Carracci (1557–1602); Diana De Grazia suggests it is a headpiece, as it has no handle, and in her *Prints and Related Drawings by the Carracci Family* (Washington, 1979) dates it to 1595.

Spanish etched fans are even fewer in number but include a view of the Plaza Mayor, Madrid in about 1788 (see illustration p. 43).

All but two of the German fans in the Schreiber Collection are etched. An example of a German etched fan (S.M. 234 and S.F. 133), was sold in the Baldwin Collection (CSK, 4 May 1978, lot 62, £180); it depicted Frederick II in Elysium printed on silk. The three so-called Dutch fans in the Schreiber Collection are pastoral etchings, and English, but a small number of stencilled fans, including a ballooning fan in Dr van Eeghen's collection and a Dogger Bank fan in the Schreiber Collection, are probably Dutch.

It is, of course, not that easy to identify the country of origin of etched fans, even if they have inscriptions. An early 19th-century fan leaf (S.U. 237) is copied from two English drawings, or more probably the prints after them by William Williams, 'Before Marriage' and 'After Marriage'; the fan leaf is probably French but it is also inscribed in Spanish as well as French. A pair of fan leaves (S.U. 303 and S.F. 129; and S.U. 304) are French fans for the Spanish market, each with 32 flowers with their names in Latin and French and the publication lines in Paris, 'fabrica de Abanicos de Fdo. Custelier y Compia'. Another teaser is a fan, Grammaire Française à l'usage des Rentiers (see colour plate p. 63); although it is a French 'satirical fan', the Rentier is dressed in English clothes and the etching looks decidedly English.

Nor can the date of the plate be a guide to the date of the fan. The fanmaker Duvelleroy kept a stock of early 19th-century plates for his clients to choose from when they wanted old subjects. Dr van Eeghen has a fan of 1905 with a print of 1845 on it.

Aquatints

Towards the end of the 18th century aquatint, a tone process, comes in. Aquatinting is a variation of etching and produces a mass of dots rather like a watercolour wash by the use of a resin that is deposited on top of the wax. Only a few fans using this method survive, as it was rather too complex and elaborate a process.

Examples include a view of Bartholomew Fair in 1721, published by J.F.Setchel, 23 King Street, c. 1780; and Covent Garden (S.U. 104 and S.E. 45; and Christie's, 12 March 1973, lot 94, 65 gns). Six of the Peninsular War fan leaves in the Schreiber Collection are in this medium; they include portraits of Ferdinand VII and of the Duke of Wellington. Most of them are translated into Spanish for shipment out as propaganda, but a number seem to have remained in England unused, in the hoard mentioned earlier in this chapter. 'The Altar of Love', published 1808 by I.Reed, 133 Pall Mall, is also an aquatint, as is the Conundrum fan

65

Fan, the leaf a hand-coloured etching of a scene from a romance in Tudor fancy-dress, the reverse with a similar scene; the mother-of-pearl sticks painted with vignettes and gilt, the guardsticks of gilt metal chased with flowers. French, c. 1815. In double-sided glazed gilt wood frame. (Photograph by courtesy of Christie's South Kensington: 17 July 1979, lot 141, £ 160.)

(1799) (Christie's, 14 July 1969, lot 71, 32 gns). Although they used aquatints for their finest colour-prints, the French were sparing in using it for fans. In the Schreiber Collection there are three mounted fans of the Revolutionary period and an un-mounted leaf of Napoleon. There is also an Austrian aquatint fan of Emperor Francis II (s.u. 292 and s.f. 134).

Stipple Engravings

Stipple was a late 18th-century improve-ment of engraving, a method that produces broken lines of little dots, using a tool rather like a spur. It is a method fashionable under Bartolozzi.

This group of fans, together with the pastoral and theatrical etched fans, are the most common English printed fans. The next group of fans, mainly of classical or fancy subjects, are made from the same copper plates as small fancy prints and are engraved in stipple by Bartolozzi and his followers. An example was the fan sold at CSK, 17 July 1979, lot 164 (see colour plate p. 65). On these fans all inscriptions on the plate have been masked out or uninked. The engraving is usually uncoloured and the reserves are painted in with designs. Examples include 'The Theft of Cupid's Bow', engraved by F.Bartolozzi, R.A. from a design by Angelica Kauffmann, R.A. (S.U. 60); 'The Power of Love' (1780), engraved by Bartolozzi and published by Poggi (S.U. 76 and S.E. 58); 'Playing Shuttlecock' (c. 1820) (Christie's, 5 November 1974, lot 16, 28 gns; also S.U. 94 and S.E. 93); and 'Travellers', drawn by Princess Elizabeth, daughter of King George III, indefatigable etcher and pupil of Benjamin West, and engraved in stipple by H.Thielcke. There are also portraits of John Milton (S.U. 12 and S.E. 90), Alexander Pope (S.U. 13), and Charles James Fox (S.U. 16), all unsigned; that of Lt. Col. Sir Banastre Tarleton, the rich Liverpudlian soldier who is best known for his ravaging America with the Light Dragoons (the Tarleton bonnet is named after him), published on silk by I.Cock, Wood Street (1782), was painted by Thomas Stothard and engraved by Wells. Others were the Chapel fan (1796) (S.M. 56 and S.E. 141); 'The United Sisters', commemorating the Act of Union in 1800 of England, Scotland and Ireland (S.U. 36 and S.E. 26), inscribed 'Fair Sister Isles... blest as free', engraved by George Wilson and published by Ashton and Hadwen, 28 Little Britain, 1 January 1801; another example of this fan was sold at Christie's, 21 October 1970, lot 280 (8 gns). The same stipple-engraved vignettes are sometimes printed on silk cut-out and often appear on English fans at this time, sometimes applied to sandalwood brisé fans. The other principal subjects are novels and the classics.

There are several French fans engraved in stipple dating from the end of the 18th century. Mirabeau was a popular subject (S.M. 115 and S.F. 58), and early in the 19th century there is a group of charming fans often with stipple-engraved faces printed in colour and the rest of the fan painted in bright and cheerful colour with romantic and pretty scenes. They are often signed and numbered, and were produced in large quantities. By now their sticks are often very elaborate.

Printed fans are now nearly always coloured. Publishers include Vve. Garnison. By this date the printed fan had changed its function and country of origin. They are now mainly French or from other Continental countries, no longer normally uncoloured but brightly coloured, and, most important, no longer necessarily cheap fans. They are often mounted on very elaborate sticks. At the turn of the century the subjects tend to be commemorative – until about 1815 – and then throughout the Restoration essentially romantic and pretty fans appeared. The Schreiber Collection contains a single German stipple-engraved fan of King Frederick William III and Queen Louise of Prussia (1798) (S.U. 291 and S.M. 237). Dr van Eeghen has a curious printed fan: its leaf is Italian, with etched outline and stipple features of a Roman scene engraved about 1815, and coloured and mounted about 1845, probably in France; the colours (black and red) are applied without tone, and the shading is in gold.

Mezzotints

The mezzotint is the most laborious engraving process of all, involving covering the copper plate with a mass of scratches and then removing them where the engraver wishes the plate to print light. Mezzotints, although common in England, were very expensive: they cost about £1 when framed in 1760; this was because it is such a very laborious and skilled process.

Mezzotint fans are even rarer than the types already mentioned – only six examples are known: 'Departure of a Hero' (c. 1780) (Christie's, 19 February 1974, lot 30, 100 gns: see colour plate overleaf); two of Lord

Fan, the leaf a mezzotint, printed in colours and tinted by hand, of the departure of a hero, the ivory sticks carved, pierced and gilt. English, c. 1780. 10½ in. In the collection of the Hon. C. A. Lennox-Boyd. (Photograph by courtesy of Christie's.)

Mr. Neker, the leaf a hand-coloured woodcut of angels glorifying Necker and six verses, the reserves stencilled with scrolls; with wooden sticks. c. 1788. 11 in.; in contemporary box (lacking lid). Not in the Schreiber Collection. (Photograph by courtesy of Christie's South Kensington.)

Rodney, both different (one S.E. 15 and S.U. 18 – he was notoriously vain and so these were probably private commissions – the other Christie's, 7 November 1973, lot 14 (with two other fans), 50 gns); 'Unveiling a Statue' (S.U. 32); a fan with a small allegorical vignette (private collection); and 'The Night Journey' (S.U. 100 and S.E. 103), published and probably also engraved by J.Jehner, an obscure but very able engraver and painter who worked in London in about 1775, and then in Devon, returning later to publish this print in 1800; this print was originally intended as a transparency.

Woodcuts

Woodcut fans are equally rare. It is a cheap method but probably too coarse for the necessarily small scale of the object and the comparative sophistication of the market. Woodcuts produce a rather crude ink effect, not quite so heavy but the same effect as the somewhat harsh quality of a child's potato cut or a finger print.

A French woodcut fan of Necker (c. 1788) (CSK, 17 May 1979, lot 85, £160: see colour plate opposite) and one other (Christie's, 6 November 1972, lot 158, 50 gns) are the only two to have come on the market between 1968 and 1979, and a set of four curious fan designs, possibly Dutch, are the only example of woodcuts in the Schreiber Collection (S.U. 397).

Lithographs

Lithography is the most direct process. The plain surface of a prepared stone prints where the crayon is drawn over it. On fans it is easy to identify as there is a black crayon-like under-drawing and no fan painter would use crayon, which would show through the paint. Lithography,

although it comes in from the beginning of the 19th century, was most used for fans from the 1830s and 1840s onwards; they are usually printed with *fêtes champêtres* in 18th-century style and the figures, often wearing 17th-century fancy dress, were then hand-coloured. The most elaborate examples have fine mother-of-pearl sticks, the cheaper bone; the fans of medium quality tend to have ivory sticks (see colour plate). A great number of these pretty fans survive; they tend to realize about £20–£150 each, depending on quality. Late lithographs were sometimes printed on satin; there is an Italian example in the Schreiber Collection

Hand-coloured lithographic fan of figures in 18th-century dress in a landscape; the ivory sticks pierced and gilt, the guardsticks carved with roses and the handle set with turquoise. French, c. 1860. In the author's collection.

Fan, the leaf a chromolithograph of an incident during an election; with mother-of-pearl sticks. 14 in. (Photograph by courtesy of Christie's South Kensington.)

(S.M. 220) of the Duomo, Florence, by Giovanni Gilardini (No. 219). Printed fans are engraved in the method popular in the country where the print is made. For instance, the French were fond of lithography and produced quite a number of fans by this method, as it is the cheapest way of doing it.

Chromolithographs

Chromolithographs are printed from a number of stone 'plates', each in a different colour. They normally have rather a greasy glassy texture similar to that found on cigar boxes and 19th-century chocolate boxes. This process comes in the 1860s, although it had been invented long before it was first applied to fans. An unusual example with an election scene was sold at CSK, 31 October 1978, lot 72 (£210: see illustration). The prints are often arranged as vignettes within reserves of blue glazed paper.

There are fewer chromolithographic and lithographic fans in the 1870s, as there was a fashion for net and cheap lace, although some appeared printed on silk and linen in the 1870s and 1880s, and as imitation late 18th-century fans around the 1890s. There is an interesting group of 'art' lithographic fans made in 1904 as a memorial to a lithographer, Henry Monnier, by his friends, including Jacques Villon.

They made a fresh appearance in the early 20th century as amusing advertising fans – advertising mainly luxuries such as grand hotels (they were probably left at each table for dancers in the evening), restaurants and scents. They were mainly French; certainly the best designed were, such as Charles Barbier for Paquin (CSK, 31 October 1978, lot 47, £140). These included a series by the publisher Maquet, who employed well-known book illustrators such as Bernard de Monvel (CSK, 17 May 1979, lot 98, £65: see colour plate). Those advertising scents announce that they are appropriately scented, but these seem to have faded over the years, as have, not surprisingly, the late 17th-century and early 18th-century Italian fans, which are also said to have been scented. There are also examples of advertising handscreens and cockade fans. A number of cheaper advertising fans were made in Japan, often with woodcut decorations; one appeared in a sale at CSK, 17 May 1979, advertising Dutch cocoa.

Advertising fans can still occasionally be encountered on airlines, chiefly those from the Far East.

The 1978 invitation to the Royal College of Art's Fashion Show was a chromolithographic paper brisé fan (author's coll.).

It is strange how many of these late printed fans survive, often in mint condition, but they were probably kept to remind the recipient of a special evening - a romantic dancing partner or a delicious dinner – and, of course, folded fans take up very little space.

Fan, the leaf a coloured lithograph of a lady and a dog in a flying machine, advertising Parfum Pompeia, Parfumerie L. T. Piver, 10 Bould. de Strasbourg, Paris, drawn by Mich and engraved by Maquet, 10 rue de la Paix; with wooden sticks. French, c. 1925. 9¾ in. (Photograph by courtesy of Christie's South Kensington.)

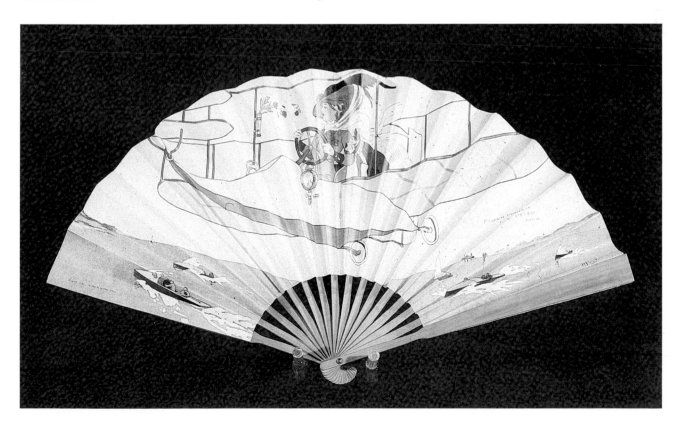

Fan, the leaf painted with a scene from a novel in the style of Stothard or Corbauld; with pierced ivory sticks. English, c. 1820. In the collection of the Hon. C. A. Lennox-Boyd. (Photograph by courtesy of Christie's South Kensington: 22 Kensington Palace Gardens sale, 12 December 1977, lot 98.)

5

Nineteenth-
and twentieth-century
Painted Fans

In the 19th century fans become more mass-produced and, on the whole, less fine in quality, but they are very decorative. Spain joined France in becoming a leading producer. Painted fans are no longer necessarily the more important fans. The painted scene is often relegated to the back of the fan and the front bears a lithograph such as one sold at CSK (Baldwin Coll., 4 May 1978, lot 22, £220), a fan depicting the Surrender at Baylen; the reverse is painted with the Maid of Saragossa, one of the heroines of the siege. General Pierre Dupont with 18000 men surrendered on 23 July 1808 to General Castanos at Baylen. Among the results of this severe reverse to the French, the siege of Saragossa, an unfortified city and the capital of Aragon, was temporarily raised. It was renewed at the end of December, the defences were breached on 27 January, although the city did not fall until 20 February after an heroic resistance. Maria Agustín, the Maid of Saragossa, is mentioned in Byron's *Childe Harold,* Canto I. This, like many other early to mid-19th-century fans, is painted very much in 18th-century style, notably in the arrangement of three vignettes on the leaf.

In the 1840s to 1860s the figures are often dressed in 18th- or even 17th-century clothes and are enjoying *fêtes champêtres* and other pastoral and courtly pleasures – the same pastoral pleasures that they enjoyed on 18th century fans.

Most of the early 19th-century fans are small ivory or horn brisé fans, some English, others possibly made in Dieppe, pierced and painted with garlands of flowers. Sometimes, however, they are more elaborate and are painted with charming vignettes such as the double-image fans to be described in Chapter 7, or the unusual fan, No. 127 in the Madrid Exhibition in 1920: this is rather an odd mixture – a pierced horn brisé fan of Gothic shape painted with a chinoiserie

Fan, the leaf painted with an elegant flautist and audience and with the Arts, the reserves with shells, vines, fruit, feathers and flowers; the mother-of-pearl sticks carved, pierced, gilt and painted with fruit and blossom. The sticks c. 1760, the leaf a 19th-century pastiche. 11¾ in. (Photograph by courtesy of Christie's South Kensington: 23 October 1979, lot 154, £220.)

Fan, the leaf painted with Souls Ascending to Heaven in the style of William Marshall Craig; the ivory sticks pierced and painted with angels. c. 1790. 10¼ in. (Photograph by courtesy of Christie's South Kensington: 18 November 1976, lot 103, £110.)

frieze. Fans of this type date from the first quarter of the 19th century; there were, however, similar fans made late in the century. From the first few years of the century, there survive some fine English brisé fans, extremely well painted, probably by miniaturists, particularly those who specialized in illustrations, such as William Marshall Craig. One was painted commemorating the Act of Union of England and Ireland, 1800. In Spain and Italy during the same period (first quarter of the 19th century), there are examples of small fans, often with fine leather or chickenskin leaves and rather fine sticks, often of mother-of-pearl, with gilt metal guardsticks set with semi-precious stones. A fine example of this type of fan was No. 152 in the Madrid Exhibition (from the collection of the Duquesa de Talavera); it is painted with a palace in a park with temples – la Alameda de Osuna – within red drapes. The reverse is painted with the initials of Doña Maria Josefa Pimentel, Condesa-Duquesa de Benavente, wife of the Duke of Osuna who built the Alameda and was called 'El Capricho'.

In the 1820s and 1830s fans grew longer again and the Spanish ones, particularly, resembled 18th-century ones – even the mother-of-pearl sticks are carved and pierced in 18th-century style. Such fans were probably produced only in France and Spain.

No. 230 in the Madrid Exhibition is painted with the wedding procession of Ferdinand

VII and Doña Maria Cristina. The leaf is a full 180° and the procession winds right round the semicircle as it might in an oriental fan, but an uncommon occurrence in European fans.

Now more amateur artists are embellishing their own fans, although they do not do so in quantity until the second half of the century.

Pairs of handscreens were fashionable in the second quarter of the 19th century. Most are of papier mâché painted with landscapes and lacquered; some are of pressed card. Many are of English origin.

By the mid- and later 19th century, most fans are hand-coloured lithographs. Only the very finest fans, at least the most expensive such as some made by Alexandre, and some of the weakest fans, often by amateurs, are now painted. From this point onwards, it is common practice for painted fans to be signed. A quantity of Spanish and French fan painters flood the scene. One fan sold at CSK was even signed by three artists, as there were painted vignettes on the sticks.

In the 1860s and 1870s fans were often painted on satin. For amateurs, Duvelleroy and the other fanmakers sold plain satin fans and ivory and wooden brisé fans to be painted with flowers and birds. Apparently, a dog's head or a favourite racehorse were popular subjects in 1886, according to the *Englishwoman's Domestic Magazine*. Some autograph fans fall into this type; they are

---

Fan, the gauze leaf painted with Prince Herman of Saxe-Weimar winning the Brown Derby, Germany, by Ch. Auront; with wooden sticks. c. 1890. 17 in. Formerly in the collection of Princess Gerta of Saxe-Weimar. (Photograph by courtesy of Christie's South Kensington: 17 May 1979, lot 68, £90.)

Fan, the leaf painted with elegant shepherdesses in 18th-century style in the manner of John Massey Wright; the mother-of-pearl sticks pierced and gilt. c. 1840. 10½ in. (Photograph by courtesy of Sanders of Oxford.)

Below: The Shadow of the Gendarme, the silk and gauze leaf painted by S. Drinot with the shadow disturbing child pierrots stealing apples over a wall, the reverse with the scene beyond the wall; with tortoiseshell sticks, one guardstick carved with a gendarme with ivory face and hands. 11 in.; in Duvelleroy box. Believed to have been designed by Richard Doyle for Louise, Lady Hillingdon. (Photograph by courtesy of Christie's South Kensington.)

normally painted on brisé fans, each stick with a small vignette and an autograph or inscription.

Until the few decades of the last century, when fans began to be signed, the anonymity of fan painters remains. In England, however, some names appear. Doyle, the caricaturist and illustrator, painted a fan which is now with the collection of H.R.H. Princess Margaret. An extremely well painted fan (Sanders of Oxford) of about 1840 is extremely close in style to John Massey Wright (1777–1866), a distinguished book illustrator (see colour plate); another by the same hand belongs to Dr van Eeghen.

Although the mainstream of High Victorian illustration – 'the illustrators of the Sixties', in James Glesson White's phrase – was in subject and treatment unsuitable for fan painters, there were painters whose work could have been adapted for the fan. But we must wait until another fan can be identified.

On the Continent, illustrators mainly used lithography. Unfortunately, it was rarely coloured and so the school of illustrators was, with the exception of Romantic subject painters like the Deveria brothers, far removed from fan painters, and had no such similar trade to turn to or be trained in, and so we cannot even hazard a guess under whose influence the fan painters worked.

In an attempt to improve the quality of fan painting, the Fanmakers Company launched a series of exhibitions and competitions in the 1870s. Unfortunately these were not a success.

The 1880s and 1890s saw a revival of more interesting and artistic fans. There are some superb and very amusing, often eccentric, designs exhibited in the Karlsruhe Exhibition (1891), including nude ladies on polar bear skins, and giraffes knocking putti out of palm trees. Another very amusing fan was sold at CSK 5 May 1977 (lot 198, £220: see illustration opposite) of a policeman and

children stealing apples; one of a circus, signed J. Donzel, with a clown on the guard-sticks, was sold at Sotheby's Belgravia, 1 February 1979 (£190).

Cheaper or amateurish fans could be rather ridiculous, such as the one sold at Christie's of a lady promenading her poodle along a twig.

Another type of fan of this period was often painted on gauze with lace insertions specially worked to the correct shape,

---

Fan, the black lace leaf set with a shaped silk vignette painted with lovers and putti by a gazebo; with stained mother-of-pearl sticks. Late 19th century. 14½ in.; in Duvelleroy box. Formerly in the collection of Lady Charlotte Schreiber. (Photograph by courtesy of Christie's South Kensington.)

sometimes forming objects such as gondolas, and in the case of this pretty fan from Lady Charlotte Schreiber's collection a gazebo (CSK, 17 May 1979, lot 89, £230: see colour plate on previous page). They can sometimes be viewed from both sides. The cheaper versions of this type of fan were less well thought-out, just painted with sprays of flowers or butterflies interspersed with insertions of fragments of lace flounces.

Occasionally, one comes across rare interesting fans painted and used by aesthetes: Christie's, 24 March 1969, lot 184 (18 gns) was one such fan. The laid mount was painted with three portrait heads by a follower of Sir Edward Burne-Jones (see colour plate). The fan came from Old Battersea House, the house of Mrs Stirling, patron and collector of her brother-in-law William de Morgan's pottery, and was probably painted by her great-uncle J.R. Spencer-Stanhope, a friend and pupil of Burne-Jones.

At this period, until the First World War, almost for the first time, artists of high quality, as opposed to fan painters, are known to have designed and even decorated fans. Charles Conder designed several such fans. His fan leaves were mainly painted on silk with pretty pastoral scenes; they were considered too good to be mounted. Amongst other examples, there is one in the Ashmolean Museum, Oxford, and they pass through the London salerooms regularly, fetching about £200–£800.

Whistler and the interest in Japan from the 1870s onwards had clearly re-awakened the

An interesting fan, the kid mount painted with three portrait heads, a serpent, oranges and pomegranates, the reverse gilt and overpainted with three armorials and two pairs of badges. By a follower of Sir Edward Burne-Jones, late 19th century. 10 in.; in glazed case. Provenance: Old Battersea House. Now in the collection of the Hon. C. A. Lennox-Boyd. (Photograph by courtesy of Christie's.)

Fan, the leaf of Brussels lace worked with a coat of arms within a border of gauze painted with flowers; the mother-of-pearl sticks carved, pierced, silvered and gilt. Lace c. 1880; probably mounted c. 1900. 14 in. The arms are believed to be those of Princesse Annie de Lusignan. (Photograph by courtesy of Christie's South Kensington: 23 October 1979, lot 9, £160.)

interest in fans; although fans were no longer a fashionable accessory, the fan shape was fashionable and still used. Edgar Degas decorated fans with crayon drawings of dancers and there are examples by Van Gogh, but fan designs by artists of this calibre tend to appear only in picture sales and important art collections. In the 20th century, the German Expressionist Oskar Kokoschka painted fans; an exhibition of them was held in 1969. There were also less famous artists like George Sheringham, who held an exhibition of fans and panels painted on silk at the Ryder Gallery in 1911. In France, decorators such as Barbier were designing fans: there is a fine lithographic example of his work (mentioned in Chapter 4). Erté designed some unusual fans but one does not know how many of his fanciful designs were actually carried out. The Dutch Art Nouveau painter Willem van Konijnenburg (b. 1868) painted a wood brisé fan for a friend in 1890.

Feathers, lace, sequins and lithography were playing such a large part in the decoration of fans in the late 19th and early 20th centuries that, apart from the mass-produced cheap fans with small scenes and some bullfights hashed out by Spanish fan painters, very few painted fans were produced at that time. There were a few special commissions from important serious collectors, such as Queen Mary, the rich Haut-Bohemians commissioning fans from artists, and the French designing way-out fans to tone in with way-out clothes – such as Barbier for Paquin, Erté for himself.

Fan, the leaf painted with a pedlar, with a river and mountains in the distance; with bamboo sticks and ivory guardsticks, decorated with shubayana work. Japanese, late 19th century. 11 in. (Reverse illustrated; photograph by courtesy of Christie's South Kensington: 17 July 1979, lot 166, £ 50.)

6 Oriental and Ethnographic Fans

Chinese and Japanese Fans

Apart from different types of fan, in China from the late 17th century onwards two distinct styles were produced: those for internal consumption and those for export to Europe via Canton and India. These, in turn, can be subdivided.

Before that date one is dealing with innumerable types of fans, all for home use. The collector today is unlikely to be able to add any examples to his collection, although there are some fine early Chinese fans in museums, mainly unmounted or dismounted painted fan leaves.

The history of Chinese fan painting is the history of Chinese painting. The student of Chinese painting is not helped by the great reverence for past masters and past styles that has existed in all Chinese art. The scale and medium of painting have remained constant: brush and ink outline with faint colour washes laid on paper or silk. The subject is normally landscape – usually sublime and misty. Distance is indicated by emptiness, often subtle. This, with the diagonal composition that was the norm until late in the Yuan period, means that fan shapes, both rigid and folding, are most suitable for paintings. For many centuries there were schools of 'literati painters', rich officials who dabbled in art and exchanged paintings, poems and calligraphy. All this led to fan decorations becoming a major part of painting and calligraphy.

In Japan the reverence for Chinese forms existed from the beginning and, even if they departed from the canons of Chinese taste, they did not often stray far. They painted flowers and fish more often than the Chinese and they used bright colours when they painted people – which they did often – and they painted on gold-leaf. None of these differences interfered with their fan painting. The lack of shadows and perspective made fan composition easier, and when in the late 18th century these Western ideas crept into Japan it was the popular painters of Edo who used them; these were the artists of the block prints so famous in the West, who worked for the ordinary tradespeople of the capital. They designed prints to go on fans and in these they added perspective. A few of these Japanese printed fans survive, and a dismounted example from the Victoria and Albert Museum by Utagawa Sadahide (1807–73), depicting a seaweed gatherer, was exhibited in *Fans from the East*.

Many of the Chinese and Japanese fans for 'home' use are of the painted variety. They often survive only as unmounted or dismounted fan leaves, for both folding fans and handscreens, because it was the painting which was valued. Indeed, the sticks of Chinese fans for use in the East are normally very plain, often bamboo, as opposed to the elaborately carved and lacquered sticks produced for the European market.

There were of course a number of other types of fan made in both China and Japan

Ivory brisé fan with hairwork carving of saru examining a kanemono, one holding a peach plucked from a tree behind; the guardsticks with gilt takamakie. Japanese, late 19th century. 11 in. (Photograph by courtesy of Christie's South Kensington: 17 July 1979, lot 161, £350.)

at the time. They were mainly ethnic and chiefly handscreens.

A Qianlong (1736–95) handscreen of jade with gilt decoration from the Fitzwilliam Museum was illustrated (plate 4) in *Fans from the East*. A flywhisk in the Horniman Museum has an ivory handle decorated with strands of coloured silks with an overlay of hair. In the Victoria and Albert Museum is a pair of fine early 19th-century handscreens of tortoiseshell and bamboo appliqué with embroidery. There also exist several 19th-century folding fans with maps, more similar to European fans. The Horniman Museum contains a late 19th-century handscreen of betel palm decorated in pokerwork, and a handscreen of palm leaf with a bamboo handle decorated with tortoiseshell. Similar but simpler fans of this type are still made in China, and at the time of writing were being used for window-dressing in Peter Robinson in London and in a smart dress shop in Amsterdam.

In Japan, the *Suehiro ogi* or 'wide-ended' fan first appeared in the 15th century, but was still used in the 19th century. There were also heavy curved wooden handscreens, including those used by umpires at wrestling matches, folding fans, and handscreens with iron handles used by commanders for giving orders in battle.

The earliest Chinese export fans to survive are a small series of ivory brisé fans lacquered in red and gold with scenes with both European and Chinese figures, the reserves with flowers and beasts and the borders pierced. The example in the Victoria and Albert Museum (2256′T6) was exhibited in *Fans from the East*. An identical fan was sold at CSK, 31 October 1978, as was a similar fan. The Europeans depicted in these fans look rather strange, as the Chinese artists were not able to understand how their clothes worked. This we shall see again and again in the Chinese attempt to copy European fans or draw European figures – to please and capture the European market – as it is usually in the clothes and in the faces that they fail.

The next group of fans to survive are painted fans of about the 1780s copying English 18th-century fans with Biblical and classical scenes, such as the fan in the author's collection (see colour plate). This has mother-of-pearl sticks and is carved with initials and a date, and must have been a special commission.

Fan, the leaf painted with a Biblical scene after a European design; with mother-of-pearl sticks carved, pierced and gilt and inscribed SM 1786. Chinese. In 20th-century glazed case. In the author's collection.

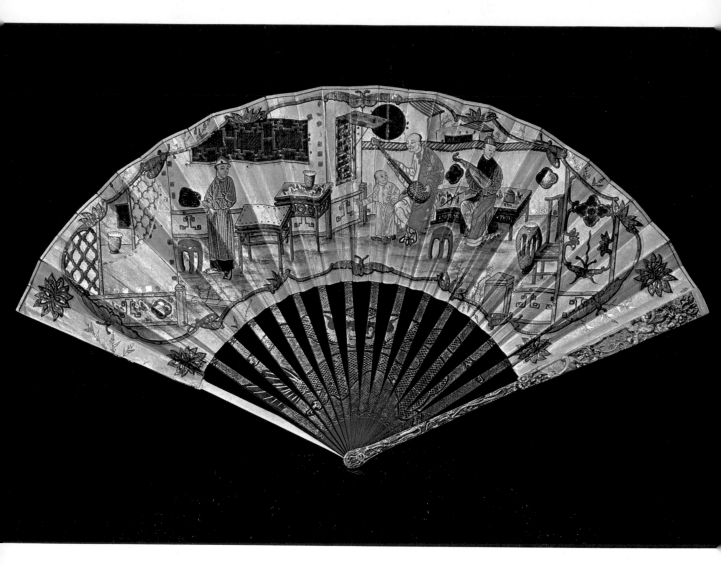

Fan, the leaf painted with musicians with painted silk faces and clothes and decorated with mica and net insertions and painted panels of mother-of-pearl, the reverse with figures in a garden; with lacquered sticks, the ivory guardsticks carved with a tree and figures, and painted and set with mother-of-pearl putti. Chinese, c. 1780. 11½ in. Now in the Victoria & Albert Museum. (Photograph by courtesy of Christie's South Kensington.)

From the same period more fans survive painted with Chinese figures in a landscape against an off-white/brownish ground, mounted on plain pierced ivory sticks with carved guardsticks. The leaves of these fans are sometimes *découpé*, possibly done later on arrival in England. These fans rather resemble the English etched chinoiserie fans of the 1740s. A good example was lot 88, CSK, 17 May 1979 (£150), which belonged to Lady Charlotte Schreiber. A rare and fine series of fans included CSK, Baldwin Coll., 4 May 1978, lot 88 (£410: see colour plate), now in the Victoria and Albert Museum. This was painted with Chinese figures with applied silk clothes in an interior; the windows are mica and net insertions and the reverse of the fan shows the exterior of the house. The sticks are lacquered and the guardsticks are ivory carved with a tree and its roots.

Another charming group of Chinese late 18th-century fans is painted with views of the European merchants' warehouses or hongs at Canton – CSK, Baldwin Coll., 4 May 1978, lot 14 (£260: see illustration) was an example. A further example in the Victoria and Albert Museum was illustrated (plate 6) in *Fans from the East,* and a similar fan in the Mottahedeh Collection in A. Du Boulay, *Chinese Porcelain* (figs. 121 and 122). The reverse of such fans is painted with flowers and fruit. It was this style of painting brightly coloured flowers, fruit, birds and figures which was to enchant Europeans, particularly the English, for the next hundred years. The colours are clear and bright

and the draughtsmanship is very precise, like that of a miniature artist.

From about the turn of the century to about 1820 one finds fans painted with these pretty birds and flowers, and with pierced ivory sticks.

From about the 1790s onwards survive a large number of pierced ivory brisé fans, at first long and narrow but getting shorter and wider by the 1810s–1820s. A thicker and clumsier fan appears after that. The later ones are often pierced with decoration against a ribbed ground rather than carved, and often have a central plaque carved with initials, again special commissions. The later

---

Fan, the leaf painted with the Hongs of Canton, the reverse with flowers and fruit; the ivory sticks pierced with flowers. Chinese, late 18th century. 11 in. (Photograph by courtesy of Christie's South Kensington.)

they are, the more Chinese figures and scenes are crowded on to the fan. There are also rarer examples of parasol or cockade ivory brisé fans with long handles. Towards the end of this period one also finds mother-of-pearl brisé fans, but these are much rarer. There were also brisé fans of cloisonné enamel, of sandalwood, and of tortoiseshell, but these, again, are rarer.

At the same time black and gold lacquer brisé fans were made. They were often similarly decorated to the ivory fans but painted, not carved or pierced, with a central shield with initials and, characteristically, an overall small motif.

From about 1820 one occasionally finds fans which resemble a brisé fan with a narrow mount attached so that the sticks take up two-thirds of the length of the fan, such as CSK, 17 July 1979, lot 177 (see colour plate).

Canton fan, the narrow leaf painted with figures in landscapes, the reverse with ladies picking flowers; the ivory sticks carved, pierced and painted in bright colours with figures in a landscape; the reverse identically carved and painted. Early 19th century. 13 in. (Photograph by courtesy of Christie's South Kensington.)

From about the 1820s we come to what, with the ivory brisé fans, are the most common of Chinese export fans: the fans applied with figures with silk clothes and ivory faces which have been known as 'Mandarin' fans. These fans were painted with scenes from Chinese life and as the century wore on they became more and more peopled. The amount of detail and number of applied ivory faces was quite a feat. The reverses, if not similarly decorated, were painted with flowers, birds, fruit and insects, sometimes on a silvered ground. The sticks were usually of pierced and carved ivory, though they are also to be found with sticks of stained ivory, bone, cloisonné enamel, lacquered wood, filigree and sandalwood. These fans were also made as cabriolet fans on occasion (see colour plate).

Cabriolet fan, the upper leaf painted with figures with ivory faces, the reverse with three painted vignettes of Chinese figures, the lower leaf painted with three vignettes of harbour scenes; with carved and pierced tortoiseshell sticks. In Canton export style, but possibly European, c. 1830. 10¾ in. (Photograph by courtesy of Christie's South Kensington: 23 October 1979, lot 2, £ 125.)

Also in about the 1820s, an interesting series of fans was produced in Macao for the Portuguese market. These had elaborate allegorical painted paper mounts depicting the Portuguese Royal family. The reverses were painted with brightly coloured European flowers. They were rather long – 12½ in. – as was becoming fashionable, and had gilt filigree sticks. An example was sold at CSK, 31 October 1978, lot 44 (see illustration).

Also about 1820 the Chinese exported charming feather fans made of white goose feathers painted in bright colours with birds and flowers in the same style as the painted paper fans; they had ivory or bone sticks.

In the 1880s a number of fans with asymmetrical sticks were produced (see colour plate opposite).

Other Oriental, Oceanic, and African Fans

Between Japan and China lies Korea which was a hierarchical Buddhist state and, not unnaturally, had fans. The Pitt-Rivers Museum, Oxford has two interesting examples given by the Royal Botanical Gardens, Kew, in 1888. They are handscreens made of rays of split bamboo covered with painted broussonetia paper: one has a free swirling motif in orange, green and yellow (the Korean national colours) – very Art Deco – the other has black Art Nouveau flowers against a gold ground. Two in the Horniman Museum are painted in the Korean national colours, and bear the national emblem – one is over three feet high. All have plain wooden handles. The Koreans also had

---

Fan, the leaf painted with a vignette of Muses, gods and goddesses surrounding a knight in armour bearing the standard of Portugal, whilst the Virgin, attended by a putto bearing a crown on a cushion, points at a gazebo in which a sunburst supports the device V I for John V I, the reserves with bunches of European flowers, the reverse with a European couple inscribed Arnoff Fethice; with gilt filigree sticks. Macao, c. 1820. 12½ in. (Photograph by courtesy of Christie's South Kensington.)

Large Cantonese fan, the silk over paper leaf painted with figures with ivory faces and silk clothes, with wooden lacquer palmette sticks. Probably mid-19th century. 14¾ in.; in lacquer box. (Photograph by courtesy of Christie's South Kensington: 23 October 1979, lot 70, £200.)

folding fans. The Botanical Gardens presented one such fan to the Pitt-Rivers Museum in 1880, a plain fan of broussonetia paper with bamboo sticks; the only difference from a normal European fan is that the thick handle curves slightly.

Farther south, in Malaya and Indonesia, there is a distinctive type of fan, mainly pear- or leaf-shaped handscreens of buffalo hide painted in gold with dancing figures and with horn sticks. Although solid they are translucent, and rather decorative. Folding examples are much rarer but do exist (see colour plate overleaf; CSK, 23 October 1979, lot 24, £50), mainly from Sumatra.

Indonesian fan, the folding leaf composed of shaped buffalo hide panels painted with dancers; with wooden sticks. c. 1850. 7 in. (Photograph by courtesy of Christie's South Kensington.)

From the island of Java, to the east of Sumatra, come multiple cockade fans of palm leaf; an example is in the Horniman Museum. Another such fan comes from the island of Praslin in the Seychelles and is illustrated in *Fans from the East* (plate 46); this was identified as being made from the coco-de-mer that grows only in these islands.

In the South Sea islands fans probably achieved their greatest social importance, and some of the largest fans were made. They are almost all of woven strips of palm leaf, the shapes varying from archipelago to archipelago; the higher the status of the holder, the grander the handle. In the Pitt-Rivers Museum there is a collection of the humbler fans including a miniature fan decorated with seeds and beads from Melanesia, purchased from the Hooper Collection in 1931. In the Marshall Islands (in Micronesia) the fans are diamond-shaped; the example presented by Lieutenant Slater in 1893 had a black-and-white checked border. Farther west in Micronesia he also collected a fan-shaped handscreen in the Gilbert Islands (now Kiribati). On Nukufetau in the neighbouring Ellice Islands (now Tuvalu) Mr C.F.Wood collected a spatula-shaped fan; this had a wooden handle and probably belonged to someone of rank.

Another fan with a carved handle is in the Horniman Museum and comes from Mangaia in the Cook Islands. It is kite-shaped and has a small 'W' notch on the tip; the wooden handle is carved with the *tiki tiki* pattern. A humbler version with plain handle, but much larger ($32\frac{1}{2}$ in. long) and with a long plaited carrying-thong, was sold at Christie's, 19 June 1979 (lot 174). The Horniman Museum has a Samoan fan with triangular leaf and zig-zagged upper edge, and also a Tahitian fan, long and triangular with a kite-shaped wooden handle with a hole in it.

These palm leaf fans are extremely rare because they rot. Although many ethnographic collections have the carved handles from the royal fans, when the fans survive with their handles we have some of the most valuable fans in existence. In the Polynesian Marquesas Islands the fans are triangular and three examples with carved handles have been sold at Christie's, the last, the cheapest, having an ivory handle made from the remains of a harpoon head.

The most valuable South Sea fan was the Reverend John Williams's fan, sold at Christie's 19 June 1979 (lot 146, £38,500: see colour plate p. 93). Not only did it have most of its leaf and the rarest of handles – the Janus figure – but it had a celebrated history. Williams of the London Missionary Society was told of the existence of the island of Rarotonga when preaching in other Cook Islands, but was unable to find it. At the same time the islanders had heard of Christianity from a Tahitian convert. One of their kings, Makea, set out to find the missionary. He found him in 1823, a disappointed explorer, and was able to set him on the right course and later help him in converting the islanders. In order to show Christianity's superiority, the various kings burned their idols and feasted off the food cooked in the ashes, and so only the fans and handles survive. It is thought that Makea gave Williams this fan.

In this case the price was due to the rarity of anything surviving from this particular island; another fan or fly-whisk handle from Rarotonga (19 June 1979, lot 145) also fetched £38,500, despite having neither its fan nor the fascinating provenance of the other piece.

From the Banks and Torres Islands of Melanesia come oblong flag-shaped fans of split and plaited palm leaf.

In some other South Sea islands fans are of lesser importance. In Fiji, a ping-pong-bat-shaped fan of decorated palm leaf with string handle was collected by Lieutenant B.E.T. Summerville in 1896 and presented to the Pitt-Rivers Museum, and the British Museum has a pierced wooden fan from Tonga, illustrated in *Fans from the East* (plate 61).

In India, fans were less important but (not surprisingly in a sub-continent) they show great diversity. A large number of Indian fans are side-mounted and revolving fans. In the Naga Hills near the Burmese border they are plain. In Indore they are of woven plaited straw.

In Peshawar (now in Pakistan) they are axehead-shaped and embroidered. Some fans from Bombay are decorated with beads and tinsel, others are of cotton embroidered with sequins and beetle wings. From Madras, on the opposite coast, come some very curious fans. One, over three feet high, in the Pitt-Rivers Museum is made from bussa palm; the handle is formed by the thicker part of the stem, and where the stem becomes the leaf, it is twisted to the side and plaited.

A fan from Madras in the Horniman Museum is large, almost circular, and made of bamboo painted with peafowl: the handle is of lacquered wood and has a ring-shaped insertion at the bottom of the fan. The fan was originally edged with peacock feathers. A much simpler example is in the Pitt-Rivers Museum. A fan from Calcutta in the Horniman Museum is circular, made of paper decorated with straw-work and fringed with dried grass.

In neighbouring Burma large fans are made of pleated bamboo. They are leaf-shaped and have curved handles mounted diagonally – the one in the Pitt-Rivers Museum was collected by the Reverend A.H. Finn in 1888. A simpler example of palm leaf with a plain wooden handle is in the Horniman Museum; these fans screened the priest's face when he preached to women. Other fans were made in Burma for export, including folding satin fans – one painted with a procession was sold at CSK recently – and also brisé fans folding to form a parakeet, as illustrated in *Fans from the East*.

To the west in Persia, leaf-shaped handscreens were made of papier-mâché and painted like the pen boxes one often finds there. Similar fans were made in India under the Mughals and later under Persian influence.

In Africa and South America there is great diversity, although fans are less common than fly-whisks. These latter predominate in South and East Africa and exist in West Africa as they do in India and elsewhere. From Madagascar, off the east coast, come grass-work fans, and farther north, in the Arab settlement of Zanzibar revolving fans were made with axehead-shaped mounts profusely covered with brightly coloured beadwork. From West Africa come circular or leaf-shaped fans on wooden sticks. The Pitt-Rivers Collection is rich in Nigerian fans and includes two hide fans, one from Kano in the north and the other from Lagos in the south – used by the wives of chiefs

to fan flies from their husbands; also a circular raffia fan from Ikot Ekpene collected in 1932 by J.F. Ross. A semicircular fan in the Pitt-Rivers Museum, given to them in 1913, is applied with cloth decorated with a trellis of braid, held in place by studs edged with ostrich feathers. Nigeria also produced interesting coloured woollen flag-shaped fans. The Horniman Museum has two hide cockade fans as well as a leather fixed fan of fan shape trimmed with feathers to make it over three feet wide, and from the Cameroons, Nigeria's immediate neighbour to the east, a beadwork circular fan with a large feather fringe.

The Pitt-Rivers Museum also has two other West African fans of typical type. One, a great curiosity, is of wood carved all over and probably used in ritual dance; it is probably well over 100 years old as it was transferred to the Pitt-Rivers Museum from the Ashmolean in 1886, having arrived earlier from the Christie collection. The other is probably not so old, but both leaf and handle are of black and white cow-hide and the leaf-shaped mount is applied with motifs of green and white leather.

The North American Indians mainly use feather fans, sometimes swan's wings, but a bat-shaped fan in the Horniman Museum was decorated with porcupine quill-work flowers and originally edged with rushes.

In the hottest parts of South America birds are abundant and there fans are made of feathers, but in the Cayapas River district of Ecuador lozenge-shaped twill-work fans were used to feed charcoal fires, in the same way as the Spanish and Portugese twill-work fans were used.

The only European ethnic face fans are the Madeira cockade fans of fine dried grass.

Of course this brief survey only outlines the types of fans from Africa, India and the South Seas. The enthusiast should direct his attention to the many books on individual tribal cultures.

Right: Rarotonga fan, the leaf of woven palm leaves; the wooden handle carved at the top with a Janus figure. Handle 13½ in. long.
Rarotonga wooden fan or fly-whisk handle carved as a male figure; 4⅞ in. long. From the James Hooper Collection. (Photograph by courtesy of Christie's.)

Four views of a double-image fan. English, c. 1820. 6 in. (Photograph by courtesy of Christie's: 7 November 1974, lot 23, 100 gns.)

Novelty

On the whole, novelty and trick fans appear in greater quantity during the later part of our period. This is, of course, because these fans were intended as amusing presents rather than lasting treasures – although this is not always so.

DOUBLE-IMAGE FANS

The earliest are the double-image fans. There is a fine example in the Musées Royaux d'Art et d'Histoire, Brussels (7768–1944), painted with classical scenes and flowers on a dark ground with tortoiseshell sticks, probably French, c. 1700. A much simpler and later example painted with figures in a landscape (c. 1770) was sold at CSK in the Baldwin Collection, 4 May 1978, lot 54 (£240). As one opens the fan the normal way one sees a lady and gentleman sitting in a garden; opening the other way reveals a moneylender and on the reverse a vignette. Some fans conceal four separate views such as the parasol fan in Wisbech Museum, described more fully under Parasol Fans: the trick is that each stick supports a double fold and a different section is extended depending upon the direction in which the fan is opened.

This method has also been used to conceal risqué scenes such as Mr Martin Willcock's fan (illustrated Gostelow, Fig. 106 and *Fans from the East*, plate 1; Chinese, late 19th century), known as a *double-entente* fan:

When opened in the normal manner to the right, the fan depicts a lady and attendants in a garden, but when opened to the left, it reveals titillating scenes (as does CSK, 31 January 1980, lot 85).

Brisé fans, too, can be double-image fans. In these the blades are deceptively wide and overlap halfway so that half the picture is painted on each half of the stick, and again, depending upon which way the fan is opened, they show a different scene. They first appear in England on sandalwood brisé fans of the 1780s and 1790s. The scenes are often applied stipple engravings and they are usually threaded with pretty green and pink striped ribbon. Then about the 1820s a charming group of pierced ivory or horn brisé fans appear, probably also English; they have pretty, brightly painted fancy scenes, on a plaque in the centre of the fan, such as baskets of flowers, a huntsman, or children (CSK, 23 October 1979, lot 35, £180: see colour plate overleaf). Like the foregoing fans, they closely resemble other normal fans of the period and so are very much trick fans which can easily deceive the inexperienced collector, who might pass them by undiscovered.

ARTICULATED

The next group of trick fans involves the sticks rather than the leaves. In about the 1770s there is a very rare group, probably produced in Germany or possibly France, with articulated sections in the guardsticks:

Pierced horn double-image brisé fan, painted with a basket of flowers and other vignettes. c. 1815. 6¼ in. (Photograph by courtesy of Christie's South Kensington.)

a metal lever is cunningly concealed in the *rocaille* and when this is pushed up or down the sections move up and down showing different faces or, if articulated, figures wave or offer bunches of flowers (CSK, 29 July 1976, lot 34, £140; Christie's, 14 July 1969, lot 94, 85 gns, and 21 October 1970, lot 302, 220 gns). There is also one in the Victoria and Albert Museum where three female heads are exchanged for three male on a lacquered slide, possibly the same fan as that exhibited in the Karlsruhe Exhibition in 1880 (p.11; collection of H.R.H. Erbgrossherzogin Pauline von Sachsen-Weimar). Another example was sold at CSK, Baldwin Coll., 4 May 1978, lot 98 (£800: see colour plate opposite): an articulated fan celebrating the birth of the Dauphin (1781); the levers raise a figure of Cupid and the crowned escutcheon of France.

There is also a trick or puzzle fan, possibly Chinese, c. 1780, where the ivory guardsticks have little channels or tracks carved in them slotted with ivory balls which run up and down as the fan is tipped (CSK, 27 May 1976, lot 7, £40).

CARVED STICKS

Another type, which really belongs to the Rococo period and was treated in Chapter 2, are especially Spanish and Portuguese 18th-century fans, whose handles are carved to form elaborate shells, sunflowers and other novelties when closed. This, in the case of Spanish fans (or rather fans for the Spanish market) and Portuguese fans, involves the carving continuing down the side of the closed fan like a fore-edge painting (see illustration p. 42).

(see illustration p. 42).

SPY HOLES

In some versions spy holes are the eyes of a mask. There is a group of interesting printed fans, c. 1740, of which several are known, including lot 18 from the Baldwin Collection, illustrated on p. 53; another is in the Boston Art Gallery and the third in a private collection. These show a face surrounded by views from Spanish life, including a fan shop and a music shop. As two of these fans, and the painted version in the Metropolitan Museum of Art all come from America, one could suggest that even though there was an English export trade in fans to Spain, they were made for the Asiento, or annual ship to Spanish America, established by the Treaty of Utrecht.

Articulated fan celebrating the birth of the Dauphin, the silk leaf painted with the Dauphin in a cradle guarded by an angel, flanked by vignettes of putti riding dolphins and busts of his parents, the reserves painted with flowers and dolphins, decorated with ribbon-work and spangles and inscribed Vive le Roy la Reine et Monseigneur le Dauphin; the ivory sticks carved, pierced and painted with the Dauphin and his nurse, fleur-de-lys and dolphins, the guardsticks set with mirrors and carved with dolphins, concealing levers which, when moved, raise a figure of Cupid and the crowned escutcheon of France. French, c. 1781. 11 in. (Photograph by courtesy of Christie's South Kensington.)

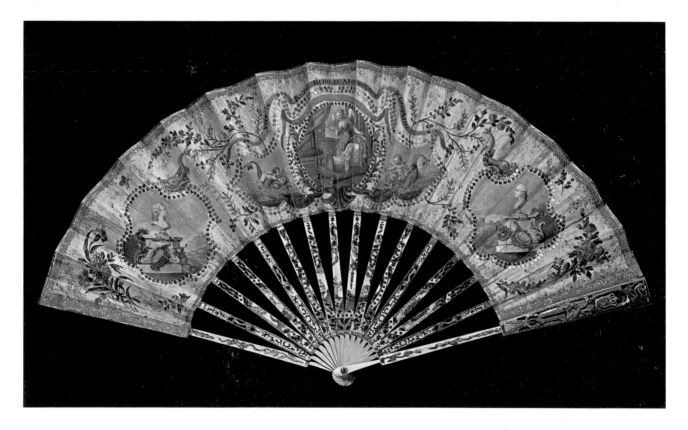

From about 1760 there appeared fans with net spy holes set in the leaf (Christie's, 27 May 1970, lot 258, 22 gns), partly decorative and partly a useful novelty. Spy holes are usually disguised as part of the design, as in some of the Swiss fans made at Winterthur (see illustration p. 47).

A Victorian version was sold at Christie's, 9 April 1974 (lot 26, 32 gns). This was a masquerade fan, the net leaf with a masque, the wooden guardsticks set with a mirror and an *étui* containing scissors, a boot-hook and a pencil (by W. Thornhill & Co., $14\frac{1}{2}$ in., c. 1880).

There is another equally well-fitted fan but without the masque, patented by W. Thornhill, c. 1895, and illustrated (plate 42) in Mrs de Vere Green's collection. The thick wooden guardsticks contain secret compartments with a comb and manicure implements in one side and sewing tools including scissors in the other, and the thimble in the tassel hanging from the rivet. So handy for running repairs! The photograph also shows an ivory brisé fan with mirror and powder compact in one guardstick. One often finds a looking-glass on guardsticks of fans – particularly Spanish lithographic fans of the mid-19th century. Rimmel's Cassolette Fan has a container for rouge on the guards (cat. No. 217, *The World of the Fan*, Harris Museum, 1976). A rare 18th-century fan sold at Sotheby's Belgravia, 5 July 1979, has a secret panel in the guardstick.

Fan, the leaf printed with a classical scene ; the ivory sticks pierced and with a watch by Upjohn set in the pivot. (Photograph by courtesy of Christie's.)

But to revert to spy holes. There is an example of spy holes in the sticks of an 1830 stipple-engraved fan with mother-of-pearl sticks (see Mrs de Vere Green's book, plate 39). Later on, in about the 1820s, spyglasses were sometimes set in the pivot of fans, often brisé, sometimes parasol brisé fans. Later in the 19th century there is even an instance of a pair of opera glasses attached to the rivet of a fan (see Mrs de Vere Green, plate 42). No. 225 in *The World of the Fan* exhibition at the Harris Museum is a similar fan (c. 1885).

In the 1760s to 1780s a spate of fans appear with novelties in their pivots or on their guardsticks, such as the superb fan of c. 1755 which has a jewelled watch by Upjohn of London, signed No. 248, as a pivot (see illustration opposite: 750 gns), and a similar fan from the collection of the Dowager Marchioness of Bristol illustrated by Woolliscroft Rhead (plate 153). The guardsticks on these fans are also jewelled, as they would have been used at court and the very grandest court fans of that period had jewelled guardsticks since, in the presence of royalty, it was customary to hold fans closed, and thus the jewelled guards presented a very grand appearance (Christie's, 7 November 1973, lot 19, 420 gns: see colour plate). No. 227 in the exhibition *The World of the Fan* was an Edwardian version of a watch on a fan: an ostrich feather fan with a watch on the guardstick.

There is an amusing fan in the museum at Bordeaux with a thermometer set in the guardstick to test one's ardour (like those modern novelties, 'passion testers', for which one clasps a phial of coloured water which changes colour if the hand is hot enough); a similar fan was sold at CSK, 17 July 1979 (lot 150, £700: see colour plate).

TELESCOPIC

Telescopic fans first appear in the middle of the 18th century. These are fans with paper leaves only loosely tipped on to the sticks. They have to have thick double mounts, so their slightly bulbous appearance may give them away. Examples include one sold at Christie's, 12 March 1973, lot 88 (120 gns), a telescopic fan painted with a fairground scene, and ivory sticks, 6½ in. expanding to 11 in. (French, c. 1760), and another (lot 93 in the same sale: see below), in its original short box by Clarke. These are normally rather crudely painted, with plain ivory sticks. To fold them when lightly closed one holds the handle and gently pushes the leaf down (very gently, as over the years they have often come out of true); the leaf then comes down to cover about half the length of the sticks and produces a neat closed fan, rather bulky, but of about the length of a small brisé fan that can easily fit into a reticule for travelling. These have

Fan, the leaf painted with the Arts, the reverse with a tree in blossom; the ivory sticks pressed with further vignettes of the Arts, the guardsticks elaborately carved and inscribed Duflos fesit, London 1778, and carved in high relief with putti, globes and other astrological instruments, one guardstick set with a Celsius thermometer. English, 1778. 11 in. long. (Photograph by courtesy of Christie's South Kensington.)

Telescopic fan, the textured leaf painted with sprays of flowers; with ivory sticks. In contemporary hexagonal box by Clarke. In the collection of the Hon. C. A. Lennox-Boyd. Photographed open but not extended, to show how strange telescopic fans look if not extended (photograph by courtesy of Christie's.)

appeared with their original short boxes which is a quick way of discovery (Christie's, 12 March 1973, lot 93, 105 gns: see colour plate). One such fan must have fallen into the hands of someone who had not understood it and had glued it up to its extended state. Lithographic versions of the 1840s also exist, as do plain linen ones of a little later, and there are examples which have strayed from turn-of-the-century fitted handbags.

CABRIOLET FANS

In the 1760s cabriolet fans were fashionable in France. These were named after the little English cabriolet carriage in vogue at the time, as their double mounts and sticks resembled the spokes of a section of a large cabriolet wheel with its reinforcing circle across the spokes. Some very fine examples exist. A cabriolet is often incorporated in the design (CSK, 29 July 1976, lot 36, £560: this fan also has a fore-edge painting of bag-

pipes, extremely rare in fans). Cabriolet fans are much sought after by collectors. They disappeared from fashion with the cabriolet but reappeared in the 19th century, when there are examples from Canton (see colour plate p. 87) and some lithographic fans.

In the late 18th century, there are some rare French Royalist fans. One is painted with Cupid with a magic lantern throwing on the screen the picture of a pansy which, when

Ivory brisé fan carved in the form of an arrow, the tips decorated with the Altar of Love, birds and flowers applied with feathers, silks and velvets. Early 19th century. 6¾ in. Photograph by courtesy of Christie's South Kensington: 23 October 1979, lot 141, £110.)

Right: Fan, the leaf painted with elegant bird-catchers sitting on a hillock with a lake beyond; the ivory sticks stained with symbols of love, clouté with mother-of-pearl and inscribed with amorous mottoes. Walloon, c. 1760. 10 in. (Photograph by courtesy of Christie's South Kensington.)

held against the light, shows concealed portraits of Louis XVI and Marie Antoinette and the Dauphin, the pansy being a transparency (see Karlsruhe Exhibition catalogue, ill. 13; collection of Frau E. Fuset). There is a similar fan in the Schreiber Collection (S.M. 123), 'Le Songe': a woman sleeps by a tomb in a rocky cemetery and again, if one holds the fan up to the light, a figure of Louis XVI stands on the grave. One of the Bastille fans in the Schreiber Col-

lection has wooden guardsticks carved and pierced as a simplified version of the Bastille.

In about 1820 an ivory brisé fan was carved to close in the form of an arrow (CSK, 19 August 1976, £38).

Two amusing late 19th-century fans were sold at CSK in 1977 and Sotheby's Belgravia in 1979. The former has sticks that fold up to become a policeman, and the latter a clown. The policeman opened to show a policeman's shadow on an orchard, and numerous boys fleeing over a wall; the reverse showed the other side of the wall and the boys tumbling off (see illustration p. 76). A similar idea occurs on certain Chinese 18th-century spy-hole fans (see colour plate p. 84), where the spy-holes are windows and their pictures show inside and outside views. This amusing idea also occurs on other late 19th- and early 20th-century fans; there are some good examples by Duvelleroy in the Victoria and Albert Museum.

Erté (Romain de Tirtoff) (b. 1892) designed some strange fans including two which appeared in *Harper's Bazaar* (February 1922); they are both disguised as long tassels to hang from the wrist – one opens to become a brisé fan of lacquered wood with gaily coloured silk strands hanging from it, the other is of jet beads. The tailpiece to the Foreword of his autobiography *Erté Fashion* (1972) is a feather parasol fan that doubles as a parasol when the feathers are swivelled to a horizontal position by pressing a lever in the long handle.

From the 1780s until about 1800 printed fans, described more fully in Chapter 4, were the main source of many novelty fans, for example 'L'Oracle', the horoscope fan with an ivory arrow-shaped pointer, and several with conundrums (S.M. 202, 203, 204, 205, 206 and 207), one being published by Sarah Ashton in 1794. Such fans were also produced in France (see illustration p. 58) and

with rebuses; S.M. 154 is a hand-coloured etching, 'Charades Nouvelles', engraved by Benizy.

Jokey fans such as 'Fanology' (S.M. 125 and S.E. 98, 99; 1797) fascinated late fan collectors; Duvelleroy even published a leaflet called 'The Language of the Fan' (see Gostelow, fig. 43), and Addison in the *Spectator* (102, 27 June 1711) satirically describes an imaginary academy for training the young in the exercise of the fan. Taken within reason, these suggestions make sense, as it is important for fans to be handled gracefully! The present generation is, of course, out of practice!

On the other hand some fans have amusing details on their sticks, such as two charming Flemish fans, their ivory sticks painted with amorous mottos and vignettes (CSK, Baldwin Coll., 4 May 1978, lot 13, £320: see illustration; the other is in the Musée des Arts Décoratifs: see Gostelow, fig. 49).

PARASOL AND COCKADE FANS

Wisbech Museum possesses a very rare, probably unique, double-image parasol fan; it is probably Flemish and dates from the early 18th century. The divided linen leaves are painted, first with crippled beggars in bright colours; the second set with scenes with gods and goddesses, also in bright colours; the third with Cupid and other figures standing in individual landscapes and hillocks and bearing symbols of gods painted in monochrome in brown; the last set is painted with similar figures in monochrome in blue bearing symbols of the Arts and the vintage. The sticks are ivory, the thick guardsticks of pierced and painted wood, one set with a circular mirror. The Victoria and Albert Museum (to whom it is, at present, on loan) suggest that it may have been a Christmas or birthday present to someone born at that time of year as poverty and disfigurement are symbolized by Saturn, the ruling planet.

In about the 1880s there is a group of very cheap-quality cockade or parasol fans, sometimes only opening to a semicircle, and also known as dagger fans, as the cockade is contained in a spatula-shaped wooden sheath. There are cords at each end. To open the fan one pulls the top cord and up snaps and unfurls the fan; to close it again one pulls the bottom cord and the fan slips back into place. The case is often inscribed 'Ricordo' and set with a looking-glass on the side. In January 1980 CSK sold a much finer example (c. 1840).

Another type unfolds from velvet- or American cloth-covered sticks, rather like certain Christmas decorations or an old-fashioned pair of nutcrackers in reverse.

Multiple parasol fans also occur. One with as many as four parasols or cockades on sticks of decreasing size was sold at CSK, 17 May 1979, lot 66 (£40); this is said to have come from Zululand.

There are other imaginative types of parasol fans. One, by B. Days, Snow Hill, Birmingham (CSK, 26 January 1977), folds into Gothic candlestick-like ornaments decried by A.W.N.Pugin in *Contrasts*. There are also some late 18th-century versions of green silk with curved wood and ivory handles, and Canton ones of pierced ivory that sometimes come with their own hanging boxes (see Mrs de Vere Green's book, plates 15 and 16).

CSK have sold several French fans decorated with cloth flowers which fold in a circular manner to form a posy (see illustration).

Fans of unusual size

DOLL'S FANS

From about 1870 until the late 1880s Paris was producing expensive bisque-headed dolls complete with trousseaux of adult clothes in trunks. These trousseaux usually included a fan, either ivory or bone brisé or satin, with painted ivory or bone sticks about an inch or so long. There also exist some slightly larger fans, often lithographic, dating from the turn of the century, which, being miniature, are said to have been made for children. They are often by Duvelleroy and other well-known makers. Perhaps they were given to clients' children, encouraging their mothers to buy the more expensive fans. These miniature fans are all fairly rare and much sought after by collectors. For the former type, fan collectors, of course, have to compete with keen doll collectors. Small fans for children are also thought to have been made in the 18th century.

GIANT FANS

Giant fans were also produced in France in the 1740s and 1780s, mainly of decorated paper, though a few were printed; they all had wooden sticks, occasionally painted. They appeared again about the 1880s, and were sometimes used as firescreens by the Aesthetes (see ill. of Norman Shaw's house in Mark Girouard's book *Sweetness and*

Light). There is another in the collection of H.M. the Queen at Osborne House: it is 27 in. long (58 in. diameter) and was painted with roses by Queen Victoria's grand-daughter Ella of Hesse (see Gostelow, fig. 80). There were also giant Japanese fans produced at the time including some sold at CSK. There is a giant fan in the Messel Collection, and two others appear in a late 19th-century photograph of M Hervé Hoguet's eventailliste's shop (Mary Gostelow, fig. 97).

Another small type of fan is the dance programme fan, sometimes an ivory brisé fan with a pencil slotted into one guardstick.

Fan, the leaf trimmed with silk violets; the painted wooden sticks folding in a circular fashion to form a bunch of violets; signed with address, possibly Av. de l'Opéra. French, believed to have been bought at the Paris Exhibition in 1900. 7½ in. (Photograph by courtesy of Christie's South Kensington: 23 October 1979, lot 10, £55.)

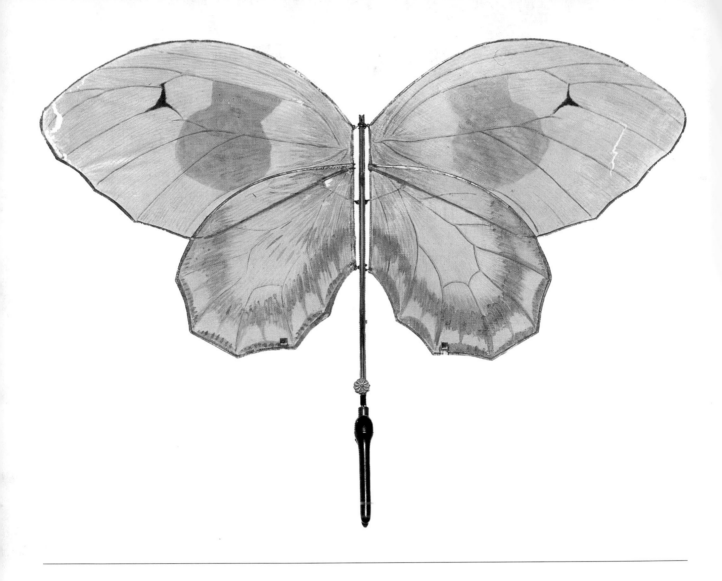

The Butterfly fan, the gauze wings painted yellow and orange with mauve veins and some gold and silver touches; with black tin handle. 23 in. wide, 18 in. long; in original cardboard box. (Photograph by courtesy of Christie's South Kensington: 17 July 1979, lot 153, £210.)

There is an example in Letchworth Museum dating from c. 1860; it is $2\frac{1}{2}$ in. long, and a corkscrew of metal on one guard holds the pencil; a gilt chain and ring are attached to the pivots to hang from the owner's finger whilst dancing. When admirers asked the owner to dance, either they or she signed the blades in advance.

At about the same time, brisé fans were often decorated with autographs, sometimes even with inscriptions, photographs and illustrations as well, and other brisé fans were decorated with collections of crests cut from letter headings and envelopes applied to the sticks. Another novelty from the 1870s was the Calendar Fan (CSK, 13 January 1977, lot 19, £4), a printed paper brisé fan. Dr van Eeghen has a chocolate box in the form of a fan, from P. Nieuwerkerk & Fils, The Hague.

A most unusual fan was included in the Victoria and Albert Museum's 1974 travelling exhibition of musical instruments. It is a parasol fan, 12 in. long – the handle formed as a violin that plays – and belonged to M Louis Clapisson (1808–66), Premier Conservateur of the Musée Instrumental of the Conservatoire.

Other novelties include Japanese daggers disguised as fans (Christie's, Bompas Coll., 14 July 1969, lot 60); brisé fans made of Welsh slate (Welsh Folk Museum); an American tinware handscreen fan moulded with pleated leaf, probably New England (Sotheby Parke Bernet, 3 February 1979, lot 1036 (with two other similar items), $650).

Mrs de Vere Green describes broken or trick fans as a Chinese invention. The plain folding fan opens normally from left to right but when handed to an unsuspecting person who opens it the other way, the fan falls to pieces. The secret is in the folding of the mount. This is made of as many pieces as the sticks and these are folded to engage with their neighbour when opened to the right, but when opened to the left the folds do not engage and fall apart. An American manu-

facturer advertised such fans for 20 cents in the 1880s. A modern version from Bali is illustrated in *Fans from the East* (plate 45).

The Craftsman of 1784 advertised Edward Vaughan's invention of the Necromantic Fan or Magic Glass Fan.

Mrs de Vere Green has also discovered another rare type. An example of this is illustrated in *Fan Leaves* (The Fan Guild), plate XXIV. This is a Panorama Fan (French, c. 1830); a rectangular handscreen with a central rectangular gap holds the panorama. This is rolled round ivory-handled spindles arranged vertically within the thickness of the fan. Small turned knobs protrude below the lower edge of the fan at either side of the handle; they draw the pictures to and fro, depending on which way they are turned. Yet another unusual type is the revolving or roll-up fan of Japanese origin, known as *Maki uchiwa*. A slender bamboo handle is slotted for most of its length and into this slot fits the circular mount, consisting of a large number of slender bamboo strips glued to a paper or silk backing in such a way that the mount can be rolled up like a blind. When the mount is slotted in the handle it is secured by a central pivot. By rotating the fan 90° it can be rolled round the handle and tied down.

Another unusual fan mentioned by Mrs de Vere Green is made of hard black rubber. When the handles were rotated it opened out into a circle, $9\frac{1}{2}$ in. diameter. This was patented by Henry B. Goodyear, the tyre magnate, in 1858. The fan had nine leaves. An example survives in the Doble Collection, Boston.

Mrs de Vere Green also illustrates (fig. 48) 'The Pedal Zephyrion' (c. 1878), a fan attached to a rod, on pedestal-like and standard lamp-like protruding pedals. The lady reader sitting beside it is able to fan herself by pedalling.

A delightful English invention has survived: 'The Butterfly Fan' (see colour plate opposite), provisional patent No. 14726.

Three examples were sold at Christie's South Kensington, 17 July 1979, lots 151–153. The gauze wings are mounted on wire frames, the handle forms the body, with a lever which when pressed closes the wings.

Feather Fans

In about 1880 feather fans returned to fashion. Painted goose-feather Canton fans had, of course, been on the market in the 1830s and 1840s but feather fans had not been really popular in Europe since the 17th century (see handscreen in Lady Rosse's collection). They remained in use until the 1930s as Court presentation fans of curled white ostrich feathers. In the 1890s feather fans often consist of simulated birds' wings. In the 20th century more and more ostrich feathers were used. They were imported from South Africa, curled and mounted on tortoiseshell, mother-of-pearl, simulated amber, ivory or wood sticks, depending on the quality of the fan. Many have survived in pristine condition in huge satin-lined fitted boxes by Duvelleroy and others. In the 1920s and 1930s they were dyed beautiful colours, sometimes shaded or streaked. Sometimes extra feathers were attached nimbly by hand to the tips of individual feathers, making the fans immensely long and producing a 'waterfall' effect. Sometimes on very expensive fans the mother-of-pearl sticks have been tinted blue, pink or yellow to match the dyed feathers. The owner's initials have often been attached to one guardstick in silver, gold and occasionally large diamonds.

There were also some small tortoiseshell brisé fans tipped with peacock and other feathers about 1890. At the lower end of the market, Sears, Roebuck & Co., a Chicago mail-order store, advertises in its 1902 catalogue:

No. 18R 989. Genuine ostrich feather fan, new size, made of fine quality stock, white enamelled sticks. You will find this a rare bargain at the special price we quote. Colours cream or black – Price, each 83c. If by mail, postage extra 5 cents.

This fan appears to be of a quality inferior to many of the fine examples by Duvelleroy and others that have appeared on the market recently. In England, the Army and Navy Co-Operative Society advertised 'real ostrich feather fans' in their 1924 catalogue, as mounted on a single handle, 9/– upwards,

Ditto 5 sticks   24/–,
Ditto 10 sticks   75/–.

On some of the cheaper feather fans the feathers have been applied as individual rosettes or cockades to each stick.

Another type of feather fan that appears on the market is a superbly made handscreen of gaily coloured feathers surmounted by a stuffed humming bird. These were made in Brazil towards the end of the 19th century and are often in their original labelled cardboard boxes (see colour plate).

Right: Handscreen decorated with feathers and stuffed humming birds; with ivory handle. Brazil, late 19th century; in original box with label. In the collection of the Hon. C. A. Lennox-Boyd.

A fan from the Walker Collection. Marriage fan, the paper leaf painted with children in a landscape and miniatures of an officer and his lady; with ivory sticks. French, c. 1770. (Photograph by courtesy of Christie's: 11 June 1974, lot 30, £ 460.)

Fan Collecting

There appear to have been two main periods of fan collecting: the 1860s to 1910s in England, and probably also Germany and other European countries; and in America and England the 1920s and 1930s.

The two celebrated collectors of the first period were Mr Robert Walker and Lady Charlotte Schreiber. These superb collections were both catalogued, Walker's for his exhibition at the Fine Art Society and sale at Sotheby's in 1882, and Lady Charlotte's by Lionel Cust when given to the British Museum in 1891. Mr Walker had, in turn, bought some of his collection from Sir Augustus Wollaston Franks of the British Museum. Another fan collection from this period was that sold at CSK on 29 July 1976, the property of a nobleman. This consisted of 59 superb fans, and sparked off a new wave of high prices: lot 59 in the sale – a French fan of about 1760 – realized £950. This very unusual fan had a leaf entirely covered with large mother-of-pearl panels painted with gods, mortals and putti; the ivory sticks were carved and pierced but not gilt. There were some rare 18th-century lace fans and six 18th-century cabriolet fans, considered very rare. There were also interesting chinoiserie and Chinese fans and an amusing English fan of about 1755 with figures running in a maze. This collection was certainly eclectic.

Other collectors, such as Lady Charlotte Schreiber, specialized more narrowly. Her collection was, of course, far larger – see Chapter 4 – but she was certainly more interested in the history and subject-matter of each fan than in its beauty. Much of her collection consisted of unmounted leaves. Lady Charlotte (1812–95), who married first in 1833 Josiah John Guest, the founder of what was to become Guest Keen & Nettlefold, and then in 1855 her children's tutor Charles Schreiber, was an avid collector. She kept diaries of her collecting trips or 'chasses', as she called them. Madeleine Ginsburg gave a charming talk at the British Museum about Lady Charlotte's life to members of the Fan Circle in 1979.

Another splendid collection of this generation is that formed by Sir Matthew Digby Wyatt, which forms the basis of the Victoria and Albert Museum's collection. Besides being an authority on the decorative arts of the Middle Ages, Wyatt was an expert in industrial art; in association with Prince Albert, Owen Jones and Henry Cole, he was one of the leading spirits behind the 1851 Exhibition, and a founding father of the Victoria and Albert Museum.

Another collection still in the collector's family was made by the Dowager Marchioness of Bristol. This included a superb fan painted with Hector and Andromache with jewelled guards and a watch set in the pivot, illustrated in Woolliscroft Rhead (plate 153).

It is often difficult to differentiate between noble collectors like Lady Bristol and those who have shown an interest in their inherited fans, but among the lenders to the Karlsruhe Exhibition in 1891 and the Madrid Exhibition of 1920, possibly Mr Marc Rosenberg was one of the few who had built up his collection from the start.

The post-war generation is not so well known. The best-known collection was formed by Leonard Messel and belongs to his daughter, the Countess of Rosse. He was very fond of Oriental fans but his collection also included a 17th-century mica fan and an early 17th-century handscreen.

The collection formed by Mrs Baldwin of Milwaukee was sold by her daughter Mrs Pabst at CSK on 4 May 1978; she bought well-painted fans and her collection was strong in commemorative fans. That formed by Mrs H. Bompas was sold at Christie's on 14 July 1969; this collection was very strong in English 18th-century printed fans and included several not in Lady Charlotte Schreiber's collection.

Another collection sold at auction was that made or inherited by the Duquesa de Marchena, sold by CSK in October 1977.

The big modern collectors are nearly all members of the Fan Circle, which was formed in London in 1975 (Honorary Secretary's address: 24 Asmuns Hill, London NW11 6ET). There are of course many other fan collectors but their collections are usually on a smaller scale.

In the 1880s fan prices were high, possibly higher in real terms than they are now, but by the 1920s they had fallen in price and it is only in the last five years that they have returned to the prices they were fetching at Mr Robert Walker's sale in 1882. Provenance is important too: the cachet of royal or theatrical ownership always adds appreciably to the price.

What should a new collector buy?

I would suggest browsing around a few sales before taking the plunge. As it would be very expensive to form a comprehensive collection of fans of all types and all periods, I would suggest that the collector specializes on some theme. But what theme? Collecting ballooning fans would be as frustrating as it is expensive, as ballooning collectors enter this field. It is also inadvisable to enter a field of collecting in which there are already a number of collectors; this often forces the price up without the new collector getting very many fans. The collecting of early printed fans is such a field. Not enough examples of each fan turn up to satisfy the existing collectors. The collector should also avoid specializing in a very rare field like mica fans: only two have come on the market in ten years, and only a handful of others are known.

If the collector wishes to have a small but expensive collection he could possibly collect 18th-century cabriolet, 18th-century lace, 18th-century *trompe l'œil* or early commemorative fans.

If the aim is to have a large attractive collection, pretty 18th-century painted fans of lesser importance, pretty late 19th-century fans or mid-19th-century lithographic fans should be considered.

It is best to avoid buying badly damaged fans until some knowledge has been acquired. If a damaged fan fetches little money at auction, it would probably be hard to re-sell when a better example is found. If a damaged fan fetches a lot of money, it probably means that some specialist collector has found a rarity.

An experienced collector may be able to repair and clean some of his own fans, but it is extremely inadvisable for the novice. Museum conservation departments give helpful advice. Even re-ribboning has problems: it is hard to find narrow ribbons, but members of the Fan Circle are able to order china ribbon through a London wholesaler. Fortunately for the fan-lover – and for dealers and auctioneers as well – to the collecting of fans there is no end.

List of Museums and Collections

AUSTRIA
Museum für Völkerkunde, Ringstrassentrakt, Neue Burg, 1014 Vienna (ethnographic)
Österreichisches Museum für Angewandte Kunst, Stubenring 5, 1010 Vienna (Figder Collection)

BELGIUM
Musées Royaux d'Art et d'Histoire, 10 Parc du Cinquantenaire, 1040 Brussels

FRANCE
Musée des Arts Décoratifs, 33000 Bordeaux (the Old Deanery, next door to the Prefecture, formerly the Palace)
Musée Carnavalet, 23 rue de Sévigné, 10003 Paris
Musée de l'Hôtel de Cluny, 6 place Painlevé, 10005 Paris
Musée des Arts Décoratifs, Pavillon de Marsan, Palais du Louvre, 107 rue de Rivoli, 10001 Paris (very fine collection)

WEST GERMANY
Museum für Völkerkunde, Staatliche Museen, Stauffenbergstrasse 41, 1 Berlin 30 (ethnographic and Oriental)
Altoner Museum, Museumstrasse 23, 2 Hamburg 50
Museum für Kunst und Gewerbe Hamburg, Steintorplatz 1, 2 Hamburg (Kokoschka fans)
Germanisches Nationalmuseum, Kornmarkt 1, 85 Nuremberg

GREAT BRITAIN : ENGLAND
Museum of Costume, Assembly Rooms, Bath, Avon
City Museums and Art Gallery, Chamberlain Square, Birmingham B3 3DH
Fitzwilliam Museum, Trumpington Street, Cambridge CB2 1RB
British Museum, Department of Prints and Drawings, Great Russell Street, London WC1 (Schreiber Collection)

Horniman Museum, London Road, Forest Hill, London SE23 3PQ (ethnographic)
The Museum of London, London Wall, London EC2
Museum of Mankind, 6 Burlington Gardens, London W1 (ethnographic)
Victoria and Albert Museum, South Kensington, London SW7 2RL
Gallery of English Costume, Platt Hall, Manchester
Laing Art Gallery and Museum, Higham Place, Newcastle NE1 8AG
Ashmolean Museum, Oxford (Oriental)
Pitt-Rivers Museum, Oxford (ethnographic)
Reading Museum and Art Gallery, Reading, Berks
Castle Museum, York
Many other local and country house museums

SCOTLAND
National Museum of Antiquities of Scotland, Queen Street, Edinburgh EH2 1JD (Mary, Queen of Scots's fan)
Royal Scottish Museum, Chambers Street, Edinburgh EH1 1JF
Burrell Collection, Camphill Museum, Queen's Park, Glasgow G41 2EW
Glasgow Museum and Art Gallery, Argyle Street, Glasgow G3 8AG

WALES
Amgueddfa Werin Cymru/Welsh Folk Museum, St. Fagans Castle, Cardiff CF5 6XB (slate fans)

ITALY
Castello Sforzesco, Milan
Civico Museo Correr, Procuratie Nuove, Piazza San Marco, Venice

NETHERLANDS
Rijksmuseum, Stadhouderskade 42, Amsterdam
Museum Boymans-van Beuningen,

Mathenesserlaan 18, Rotterdam (Monchy
Collection)
Nederlands Kostuummuseum, Lange Vijverberg
14/15, The Hague

SPAIN
Palacio Fernán-Núñez, Madrid (fine collection,
especially 18th century)
Palacio Real de Aránjuez, Aránjuez, near Madrid
(mainly 19th century)

SWITZERLAND
Schweizerisches Landesmuseum/Musée National
Suisse, Museumstrasse 2, 8023 Zürich

USA
Boston Museum of Fine Arts, Boston, Mass.
02115 (Esther Oldham Collection)
Metropolitan Museum of Art, Fifth Avenue and
82nd Street, New York, NY 10028 (Mrs William
Randolph Hearst Collection)

USSR
Hermitage Museum, M. Dvortsovaya
naberezhnaya 34, Leningrad

Bibliography

Allemagne, H.R. d', *Les Accessoires du Costume et du Mobilier* (Paris, 1928).

Archeological Institute of America, Monographs on Archeology and Fine Arts I: Eitner, I.E.A., *The Flabellum of Tournus*, (1944).

Armstrong, Nancy, *A Collector's History of Fans* (1974).

Armstrong, Nancy, *The Book of Fans* (Colour Library International, 1979).

Art Journal, *Catalogue of the 1851 Exhibition*, p. 313.

Art Journal (1875), p. 103.

Arundel Society, *Fans of All Countries* (1871).

Bapst, Germain, *Deux Eventails du Musée de Louvre* (Paris, 1882).

Bars, Carlos M. (with Juan Escoda), *Eventails Anciens* (Lausanne, 1957).

Bijutou Senshu, *Selected Objects of Japanese Art*, VI (1973): *Folding Screens with Fan Patterns in the Nanzeu-ji, Kyoto, Kano School*.

Blondel, Spire, *Histoire des Eventails et les notices sur l'écaille, la nacre et l'ivoire chez tous les peuples et à toutes les Epoques* (Paris, 1875).

Boehn, Max von, *Das Beiwerk der Mode* (Munich, 1928).

Boger, H. Baterson, *The Traditional Arts of Japan* (New York, 1964).

Bojani, Count F. de, *Eventails Anciens* (sale, Brussels, 20 December 1912; ill.).

Bordez, M.F., *Fabrication des Montures d'Eventails à Ste. Geneviève* (1875).

Bouchot, Henri, 'L'Histoire par les Eventails Populaires', *Les Lettres et Les Arts* (Paris, January and July 1883).

Brno, Moravska Galerie, *Sperky, vjire* (Jewels, fans and miniatures in the collection of the gallery; Brno, 1968).

Buck, A.M., *Victorian Costume and Costume Accessories* (1961).

Burges, W., 'Notices of the precious objects presented by Queen Theodolinda to the church of St John the Baptist, at Monza'. *Archaeological Journal*, XIV (1857), 8.

Buss, George, *Der Fächer* (Düsseldorf, 1904).

Catalani, Carla, *Waaiers* (Bussum: Van Dishoeck, Holland, 1973).

Cherpentier et Fasquelle, *Un Siècle de Modes Féminines, 1794–1894* (Paris, 1895).

Chiba, Reiko, *Painted Fans of Japan; 15 Noh Drama Masterpieces* (Rutland, Vt, and Tokyo, 1962).

Chü Ch'ao tso-p'in hsiian-chi (A Selection of Fan Paintings by Chü Ch'ao; Canton, 1962).

Ch'u, Family, *T'ieh-chin T'ung-chien-lou ts'ang sang chi chin (Collection of Decorative Fan Mounts in the T'.T' Collection in the Ch'ü family library of Chiang-Shu; Shanghai, 1937).*

Collins, Bernard Ross, *A Short Account of the Worshipful Company of Fanmakers* (1950).

The Connoisseur: I, pp. 92, 175 (on repair/restoration); 15, p. 84 (illus. of Marquis of Bristol's coll.); 19, p. 197 (illus.); 24, p. 213 (Mrs Beauclerk's coll. – some fans came from Saxe-Weimar and Goldschmidt colls).

Coomaraswamy, A.K., *Arts and Crafts of India and Ceylon* (1913).

Cosway, M., 'English Fans' in *The Concise Encyclopaedia of Antiques*, IV (1959), 298.

Croft-Murray, Edward, 'Watteau's Design for a Fan-Leaf', *Apollo* (March 1974).

Crossman, Carl L., *The China Trade* (Princeton, 1972), Ch. II, 'Fans'.

Crystal Palace, Tallis' History and Description of the, I (1851), pp. 214–19.

Cust, Lionel, *Catalogue of the Collection of Fans and Fan Leaves, presented to the Trustees of the British Museum by Lady Charlotte Schreiber* (1893).

Dawes, Leonard, 'The Nicely Calculated Flutter of the Fans', *Antiques Dealer and Collector's Guide* (March 1974).

Diderot, D. and d'Alembert, 'Eventaille', *Encyclopédie* (1765).

Dubose, Jean Pierre, *Peintres Chinois du XVIe*

Siècle: Wen Tchang ming et son école:
présentation et étude de quelques œuvres (éventails
et feuilles d'album) (exhibition at Galerie
Maurice, Lausanne, 1961).
Dunn, D., 'On Fans', Connoisseur (1902).
Eeghen, I.H. van, 'De Waaier en de Poolse
successieoorlog', Tijdschrift voor Geschiedenis
(Amsterdam, 1963).
Eeghen, I.H. van, 'De Amsterdamse
Waaierindustrie, ae xvIIIe eeuw', Amstelodamum
(1953).
Eeghen, I.H. van, 'De Watergraafsmeer op een
waaier van 200 jaar geleden', Amstelodamum
(1958).
Encyclopædia Britannica, 9th ed. (Edinburgh,
1879), IX.
Erler, M., 'Der Moderne Fächer',
Kunstgewerbeblatt (September 1904).
Fan Circle, Bulletin (1975 onwards).
Fan Circle in association with the Victoria and
Albert Museum, Fans from the East (1978).
Fan Guild of Boston, Fan Leaves (Boston, 1961).
Flory, M.A., A Book about Fans (1895).
Gibson, Eugenie, 'The Golden Age of the Fan',
The Connoisseur, 56 (1920), Gibson, Eugenie,
'Queen Mary's Collection', The Connoisseur, 78
(1927).
Giles, H.A., 'Chinese Fans', Fraser's Magazine
(May 1879); reprinted in Giles, H.A. Historic
China and other Sketches (1882).
Gostelow, Mary, A Collector's Guide to Fans
(1976).
Grand Cateret, John, Vieux Papiers, vieilles
images: cartons d'un Collectionneur. (Paris, 1896).
Great Exhibition, Official Catalogue of the (1851).
Green, Bertha de Vere, A Collector's Guide to
Fans over the Ages (1975).
Gros, Gabriella, 'The Art of the Fan Maker',
Apollo (January 1957).
Hallwyska Samlingen, Boskrifuande fürteckning
XXVI–XXX/Solfjadrar Minnen of personlige
upplefrelser, Redem innen Minner of almänne

handelser minnen frankrinsären 1914–1919
(Stockholm, 1937).
Hammar, Britta (Swedish), 'Fans of the 18th
Century', Kulturen, 1976; trans. Marion Maule,
Fan Circle Newsletter (9 October 1978).
Harari, Ralph A., The Harari Collection of
Japanese Paintings and Drawings (J. Hillier,
1973).
Hay, John, 'Chinese Fan Painting and the
Decorative Style', Colloquies on Art and
Archaeology in Asia, No. 5 (Percival David
Foundation, 1975).
Hay, John, An Exhibition of the Art of Chinese
Fan Painting (Milne Henderson Gallery, 1974).
Heath, Richard, 'Politics in Dress', The Woman's
World, (June 1880).
Hiroshi, Mizuo, Edo Painting (New York and
Tokyo, 1972).
Hirshorn, A.S., 'Mourning Fans', Antiques, CIII
(1973), p. 801.
Holme, C. 'Modern Design in Jewellery and
Fans', Studio (1902).
Holt, T.H., 'On Fans, their use and antiquity',
Journal of the British Archaeological Association,
XXVI (1870).
Honig, G.J., 'Wat een antieke waaier ons ken
vertellen met betrekking tot de Nederlandse
walvisvaart', Historia (1942).
Hughes, Therle, 'Lady Windermere's Fan',
Country Life (20 December 1973).
Hughes, Therle, More Small Decorative Antiques
(1962).
Hughes, Therle, 'Storm Dragons and Plum
Blossom', Country Life (15 June 1972).
Jackson, Mrs. F. Nevill, 'The Montgolfiers', The
Connoisseur, 25 (1909).
Joly, Henri, Legends of Japan (New York, 1908).
Kansas, University of, Chinese Fan Paintings
from the Collection of Mr. Chan Yee-Pong
(Lawrence, Kansas, 1971).
Kendall, B., 'Concerning Fans' The Connoisseur,
7 (1903), p. 4 (1902 loan exhibition, Società delle

Belle Arti, Florence, from colls of Queen Margherita, Duke and Duchess of Aosta, and Dowager Duchess of Genoa).

Kimura, Sutezō, *Edo Katuki uchiwa-e: Genroken-Enkyō ren (Kabuki fan prints from Edoi Genroku to Enkyō periods 1688–1748;* commentary by S.K. and S.I. Miyas, Tokyo, 1962).

Kiyoe, Nakamura, *Ogi to Ogie (Fans and Fan Painting;* Kyoto, 1969).

Kiyoe, Nakamura, *Nikon no Ogi (Fans of Japan;* Kyoto, 1942).

Ku Kung PoWu-Yuan-ku kung ming shan chi (Collection of famous fans from the Imperial Palace, I–IX ed. I Pei-chi, x ed. Shau Chang; Peking, 1932–35).

Kyoto Senshoku, *Bunka Kenkyukai – X korin-ha semmen gashū (Collection of Fan Painting of the Kōrin School),* ed. by the Society for Research into Dyeing and Wearing (Kyoto, 1967).

Leisure Hour, The, (1882), pp. 417–21.

Leningrad: Hermitage, *Zapadnoeuropaiskie veera* XVIII–XIX *vv. iz sobraniya… Ermitzha: Katalog vremennoi vai stavhi (Western European Fans of the 18th and 19th centuries in the Hermitage Collection),* catalogue of a temporary display with introductory essay by M.I.Torneus (1970).

Linas, Ch. de, 'Les disques Crucifères, le flabellum et l'umbrella', *Revue de l'art Chrétien* (1883).

Marcel, Gabriel, 'Un Eventail Historique du Dix-huitième Siècle', *Revue Hispanique* VIII (1901).

Margary, Ivan D., 'Militia Camps in Sussex 1793; and a Lady's Fan', *Sussex Archaeological Records* CVII (1969).

Mongot, Vincente Almela, *Los Abanicos; Fans of Valencia* (Spain, n.d.).

Mourey, Gabriel, Vallance, Aymer, *et al., Art Nouveau Jewellery and Fans* (New York, 1973).

National Encyclopaedia, The, V (c. 1880).

Niven, T., *The Fan in Art* (New York, 1911).

Ohm, Annaliese, art 'Fächer', in *Reallexikon zur Deutschen Kunstgeschichte* (Stuttgart, 1972).

Palliser, Mrs. Bury, *History of Lace* (1865).

Parr, Louisa, 'The Fan', *Harper's Magazine* (August 1889), pp. 399–409.

Percival, MacIver, *The Fan Book* (1920).

Percival, MacIver, 'Some Old English Printed Paper Fans', *The Connoisseur,* 44, p. 141.

Petit, Edouard, *Le Passé, le présent et l'avenir: Études, souvenirs et considérations sur la fabrication de l'éventail* (Versailles, 1895).

Powell, B.H. Baden, *Handbook of the Manufacturers and Arts of the Punjab* (1872).

Redgrave, S., Preface to South Kensington *Catalogue of the Loan Exhibition of Fans* (1870).

Reig y Flores, Juan, *La Industria Abaniquera en Valencia* (Madrid, 1933).

Rhead, G.W. Woolliscroft, *The History of the Fan* (1910).

Rhead, G.W. Woolliscroft, *The Connoisseur,* 55 (1919) and 58 (1920) (on Messel coll.).

Robinson, F. Mabel, 'Fans', *The Woman's World* (January 1889).

Rocamora, Manuel, *Abanicos Historicos y Anedóticos* (Barcelona, 1956).

Rondot, Natalis, *Rapport sur les Objets de Parure, de Fantaisie et du Goût, fait à la Commission Française du Jury International de l'Exposition Universelle de Londres* (Paris, 1854).

Rosenberg, Marc, *Alte und Neue Fächer aus der Wettbewerbung und Ausstellung zu Karlsruhe* (Vienna, 1891).

Rusconi, John, *The Connoisseur,* 18, p. 96 (on coll. of Queen Margherita of Italy).

Salwey, Charlotte M., *Fans of Japan* (1894).

Schreiber, Lady Charlotte, *Fans and Fan Leaves – English* (1888).

Schreiber, Lady Charlotte, *Fans and Fan Leaves – Foreign* (1890).

Seligman, G.S., and Hughes, T., *Domestic Needlework* (1938).

Shafer, Edward H., *The Golden Peaches of*

Samarkand (California, 1963).

Sociedad Española de Amigos del Arte,
Exposicion de 'El Abanico en España' 1920
(Madrid, May–June) (by D. Joaquin Ezqueria del
Beyo).

Spielmann, H., *Oskar Kokoschka: Die Fächer für
Alma Mahler* (Hamburg, 1969).

Standage, H.C., *Cements, Pastes, Glues and Gums*
(1920).

Standen, E.A., 'Instruments for Agitating the
Air', *Metropolitan Museum of Art Bulletin*, XXIII
(March 1965).

Strange, Edward F., *The Colour Prints of
Hiroshige* (Cassell, 1925).

'Studio-Talk: Fans', *Studio*, XXXVII (1906), No.
158; XLV (1909), No. 190.

Taipei, Taiwan, *Masterpieces of Chinese Album
Painting in the National Palace Museum* (1971).

Tal, Felix, *De Waaier Collectie Felix Tal*
(exhibition; Utrecht, 1967).

Thornton, Peter, 'Fans', *Antiques International*
(1966).

Thornton, Peter, 'Une des plus belles collections
du monde' (Leonard Messel Collection), *La
Connoissance des Arts* (April 1963).

Udstillingen ny kongensgade i til Fordel for
Selskabet til Haanderbejdets Fremme, Viften,
The Fan (Copenhagen, 1971).

Uzanne, Octave, *The Fan* (Eng. trans. 1884).

Vecellio, *Habiti Antichi et Moderni*, etc. (1590).

von Keudell, Baroness, *The Connoisseur*, 13
(1905), p. 152 (notes on coll. of Miss Moss,
Fernhill, Blackwater).

Walker, Robert, *Catalogue of The Cabinet of Old
Fans* (Sotheby, Wilkinson & Hoge, 1882).

Wardle, Patricia, 'Two Late Nineteenth Century
Lace Fans', *Embroidery* XXI (summer 1970),
no. 2.

White, Palmer, *Poiret* (1973).

Wild Wood, Joan, and Peter Brinson, *The Polite
World* (1965).

Worshipful Company of Fanmakers: Report of
Committee, etc., *Competitive Exhibition of Fans
held at Draper's Hall* (July 1878).

'X, Mme.', sale catalogue, *Objets d'Art,
éventails, Louis* XV *dentelles*, etc., Hôtel Drouet
(Paris, 1897).

*Zauber des Fächers: Fächer aus den Besitz des
Museum*, Altonaer Museum, Hamburg (1974).